LEARN SEO

Beginners Guide to Search Engine Optimization.

By Darren Varndell

2015 Print Edition
ISBN-13: 978-1503051058
ISBN-10: 1503051056

Copyright EZ Website Promotion, All Rights Reserved.
http://www.ezwebsitepromotion.com

Copyright, Legal Notice and Disclaimer

This publication is protected under the Digital Millennium Copyright Act (DMCA), the US Copyright Act of 1976 and all other applicable international, federal, state and local laws, and all rights are reserved, including resale rights: you are not allowed to give or sell this Guide to anyone else. If you received this publication from anyone other than ezwebsitepromotion.com or one of our partners it is likely you've received a pirated copy. Please contact us via e-mail at info at ezwebsitepromotion.com and notify us of the situation.

Please note that much of this publication is based on personal experience and anecdotal evidence. Although the author and publisher have made every reasonable attempt to achieve complete accuracy of the content in this Guide, they assume no responsibility for errors or omissions. Also, you should use this information as you see fit, and at your own risk. Your particular situation may not be exactly suited to the examples illustrated here; in fact, it's likely that they won't be the same, and you should adjust your use of the information and recommendations accordingly.

Any trademarks, service marks, product names or named features are assumed to be the property of their respective owners, and are used only for reference. There is no implied endorsement if we use one of these terms.

Finally, use your head. Nothing in this Guide is intended to replace common sense, legal, medical or other professional advice, and is meant to inform and entertain the reader.

Copyright ©EZ Website Promotion. All rights reserved.

Table of Contents

LEARN SEO..1
Copyright, Legal Notice and Disclaimer......................2
Table of Contents..3
Preface...7
SECTION 1 - INTERNET MARKETING.......................9
   Introduction to Internet Marketing............................9
   Create a Successful Online Business....................11
   Creating a Search Friendly Website......................13
      Keyword Research..14
      Choosing a Domain Name..................................16
      Creating your Web Pages...................................17
      Planning your Web Pages..................................18
      Website Tracking & Analytics.............................20
   Marketing a Website...21
   Free Internet Marketing..22
      Organic Search Engine Traffic............................22
      Social Network Shares.......................................23
      Natural Website Backlinks..................................23
      Web Directory Sites..24
   Paid Internet Marketing..25
      Paid Search Engine Listings..............................25
      Banner Advertising..26
      Section Summary..26
SECTION 2 – WEBSITE SEO....................................27
   What is SEO?...27
   Search Optimize Website Content..........................29
      1. Page Title Tags...30
      2. Description Meta Tag......................................32
      3. Optimized Page URLs....................................34
      4. Site Navigation..35
      5. Unique Quality Content...................................37
      6. Optimized Anchor Text....................................39
      7. SEO & Images...43

    8. Use of Heading Tags..45
    9. Other Page Content..47
    10. Create a Blog..49
    11. Search Engine Crawlers..50
    12. Using Sitemaps...52
    13. Setting Correct Language.......................................53
SECTION 3 - VIDEO SEO...54
  Introduction to Video SEO..54
  Optimizing Videos...55
    1. Video Content...55
    2. Choosing Video Titles..56
    3. Video Description...56
    4. Choosing Tags...57
    5. Video Transcripts...57
    6. Video Length...58
SECTION 4 - SOCIAL MEDIA MARKETING........................59
  What is Social Media Marketing?......................................59
  Social Networking Benefits..60
  Social Networking Sites...61
  How to use Social Media...62
  Social Media Integration..64
    Top Tip...65
SECTION 5 - OFF-PAGE OPTIMIZATION...........................66
  Off-Page SEO..66
  Links to your Website..66
    Back Link Quality...67
    Link Density & Diversity..68
  PageRank..69
    What is PageRank?..69
    Understanding PageRank...70
    Google Toolbar PageRank..71
    Using PageRank..72
    PageRank Summary..73
  Submitting Your Website...75
    How to Submit a Website URL....................................75
    URL Submission Mistakes..76

   URL Submission Sites..78
  Real World Promotion..79
SECTION 6 - ADVANCED SEO...80
  Advanced Website Optimization....................................80
  Web Page Load Speeds..81
  Authority Site Status..83
  Content Markup Ratio..84
  Website IP Address..85
  Secure Websites..86
  Legal Matters..88
     Legal Compliance..88
     Terms & Privacy Policy..89
  Internet Marketing Mistakes..90
SECTION 7 - SEO IN THE FUTURE......................................96
  Search Context..96
  Search Synonyms..97
  Mobile Search..98
  Social Search..99
SECTION 8 - TOP TEN SEO TIPS......................................100
SECTION 9 - TROUBLESHOOTING....................................105
  Black Hat Hurts!..105
  Common Mistakes..107
  ALGORITHM PENALTIES..115
     Panda Update..116
     Penguin Update..119
     Hummingbird Update..123
  MANUAL PENALTIES..125
     Identify Manual Penalties......................................125
     Checking for Manual Actions................................126
     Cleaning Up..127
     Common Manual Actions......................................127
     Recovery & Reconsideration................................133
     Reconsideration Requests....................................135
APPENDIX A - SEO GLOSSARY..136
APPENDIX B - ISO LANGUAGE CODES............................152
APPENDIX C - USEFUL RESOURCES................................155

Preface

Have you ever wanted to tap into the vast stream of FREE traffic offered by Google and other major search engines but found it too complicated or confusing? Well you are not alone.

If you have looked into Search Engine Optimization (SEO) techniques but failed to get the traffic your website deserves, you know that learning SEO can be confusing, especially for a beginner. There is a lot of "advice" available online, but much of it is out of date, too technical, or involves spammy software, techniques or services

Learn SEO: Beginners Guide to Search Engine Optimization brings you an easy to understand, step-by-step beginner's guide to search engine optimization, based on years of experience in the industry, and fully up to date for the SEO challenges that face webmasters for 2015 and beyond.

In a series of easy-to-follow tutorials you will learn how to:

- Uncover the traffic-generating, money-making keywords for your market or niche.
- Create quality content that your website readers and search engines will love.
- Search Engine Optimize your website or blog to tap into maximum traffic from major search engines.
- Use Social Media Marketing to boost your website audience, message or brand.
- Enhance the quality and speed of your website (Google loves fast sites with quality content!)
- Use dozens of effective insider optimization techniques that normally take years of learning to master.
- Troubleshoot ranking problems and penalties.

With clear explanations on every important ranking factor, and other vital aspects of Search Engine Optimization, you can improve your rankings, boost traffic, and ultimately sales by learning the straight forward SEO techniques presented in this book!

If the SEO practices you have been putting your faith in were produced prior to September 2012, you could be following outdated advice that will get your site penalized, or even removed from the Google index completely.

Google made major algorithm changes in 2011, and more significant changes in 2012, with further updates rolled out in 2013 and 2014. Google has declared war on some previous Search Optimization strategies that were accepted as standard practice for SEO prior to 2012, that could now be considered "black hat", or simply no longer effective.

Learn SEO 2015 Edition will show you what you can do safely in order to boost your search rankings, and outlines the practices you should avoid during the process of marketing your website or blog.

SECTION 1 - INTERNET MARKETING

Introduction to Internet Marketing

The last two decades have seen many changes to the way we live our day to day lives. Technology, in particular the Internet, has changed the way we locate information, communicate with each other and even shop for our weekly groceries!

As an established business, or person hoping to start a new business, the current trends in technology simply cannot be ignored. To take the view that offering your goods or services online as some form of expansion or optional business activity would be folly, sure to guarantee the failure of all but a few distinct cases, and in most of those cases it is likely that some form of online presence would have been of enormous benefit to the business concerned.

The aim of this book is to help not only those with an established online business that is not delivering the desired results, but those that wish to create a new online business presence, or start trading on the Internet, but lack the resources or skills usually only available to larger businesses and organizations to succeed on the Internet.

Seeking to pass on the required knowledge to create a successful online business, without the need for our readers to spend the next few years studying at college to learn new skills, by providing easy to read step-by-step guides that will help you navigate the immense world of Internet marketing and be successful with your online enterprise. This manual was written to help those with little formal training, or limited experience to achieve success in the online marketplace.

Also included within this publication are a number of tips and industry secrets that could benefit even the most seasoned internet marketer. Some concepts discussed in this book are done so on a, *what you need to know* basis, and as such are not covered in depth beyond the rules you should follow to achieve the best results.

We would encourage you to research further any concepts of interest using the many free resources available on the World Wide Web. This book aims to be your starting point to help you identify concepts and practices that are vital for online success, while avoiding the waste of time, resources and money associated with performing tasks that prove to be of little or no overall benefit in terms of increased website traffic or overall sales.

Create a Successful Online Business

The main ingredients for creating a successful online business would start with the creation of a quality, well planned, user friendly website. A *website* is a term given to a collection of interactive *web pages* that can be accessed via the Internet using a web browser (a computer software program for displaying and navigating web pages).

To make these pages available on the internet they must be placed on to a *web server*, a computer running special software with the task of providing access to these, and other pages available on the server, to people surfing the internet.

Many companies offer *web hosting* services that allow you to upload your website pages and make them available on the Internet. Whilst you may be tempted to opt for one of the many free web hosting options available on the web you should avoid this temptation as these services are usually over-subscribed, often contain advertising, and as you will discover later in this book, could give negative quality signals to search engines, effecting your overall rankings. Web hosting packages start at only a few bucks, can be tailored to meet your needs, and also take care of the server side technical setup. In most cases you only need to know how to *upload* (transfer) your files to the server.

How you upload your files to your *web space* varies from provider to provider. In some instances they may offer a web interface that you can access with your web browser to upload your files. In other cases your provider may expect you to upload your web pages and other associated files using *FTP* (File Transmission Protocol). To transfer your files using FTP requires the use of an *FTP Client*, a software program readily available to download for free, or purchase, from numerous sources on the Internet.

Once your pages are uploaded to your web space, and your website is available on the World Wide Web, the next task would be to make its existence known to the world using various online and offline marketing techniques. A failure to properly address these various tasks is the most common reason for many businesses failing to establish a presence online, depriving them of the opportunities that this global and expanding market has to offer.

The key to success is to tap into the source of the largest flow of internet traffic, and turn that traffic (website visitors) into leads and sales. Here is the good news; this huge source of traffic and potential sales is FREE *Search Engines*, in particular, the top three, namely; Google, Bing and Yahoo respectively. The largest alone deals with over *100 billion* searches per month, which is an astounding figure. To state this is a massive market would be an understatement.

The better news; if you carefully follow the steps, and adopt the core concepts and principles outlined in this book, a constant share of that traffic, and potential sales, can be yours, for *FREE*!

Creating a Search Friendly Website

In order to tap in to this incredible flow of free website visitors from search engines it is necessary to construct (or edit) our website to make it *Search Engine Friendly*. By placing certain vital information (keywords) in the right quantities, into various locations within our website, we can help search engines identify the topic of our site, with the aim of positioning our website within the first few results shown when a user searches for our type of product or service. For example, if we were marketing a website for a Pizza delivery business based in New York, we would want to be found within the first few results on major search engines when a user searches for a phrase such as '*New York pizza delivery*'. Reaching the number one position for a relevant search will ensure a steady stream of free targeted visitors to your website, all ready for you to turn them into sales.

The tasks involved in making a website and web pages search engine friendly are usually referred to *Search Engine Optimization*, or *SEO* for short. With the largest search engine, Google, using in excess of two hundred signals to decide upon a websites topic and relevance, the world of SEO can seem a daunting area at first.

However, not all of these signals are equal, with this manual cutting through the minefield of search optimization and presenting some insight into the most critical areas of SEO that need to be addressed on your website, concentrating on the main aspects that produce the best results and biggest impact on your search engine *rankings* (the position your site appears in search results).

Keyword Research

Keyword research is probably the single most important task that you will undertake with regards to your Internet marketing. Long before getting to work creating your website you will need to identify your target market. If you are experienced in the world of business you may well already understand this concept as the identification of the people you will try to sell your product or service. When it comes to marketing a website there is another vital layer that is just as important, to research your *target keywords*.

Keywords play an important role within Internet marketing as they help identify a particular topic or niche for a given web page or resource; for example if you were to pay to advertise your website on other sites on the web, you may well only want your advertisement to appear on pages related to the product or service that you offer. Most advertising agencies allow you to target your ads to specific keywords. If we wanted to advertise our car parts website we might opt for targeting sites that contain the word "car", "car parts", "motor parts" etc.

When developing your own website, keywords play an even bigger role. As most web traffic originates from search engines it would make sense to make our website perform as well as possible within these search engine result pages for people looking for our type of product or service, and the key to this is proper keyword research.

The first step is to identify the top words and phrases that not only relate to your services, products, business or brand, but those phrases that users are likely to actually type into a search engine when looking for the type of products or services that you offer.

Start by identifying two or three top keyword phrases that are used to search for your type of website. A keyword may be a single word, e.g. "cars", or contain several words, often referred to as *long tail* keywords, e.g. "Used car parts". Targeting long tail keywords is usually more effective as they have a more refined scope combined with less competition.

If your type of business is location based, as in our previous pizza delivery example, you would most certainly want to include your location (city, town, county etc.) amongst your targeted keywords.

All of your selected keywords must be related to your business or niche. The use of *unrelated keywords* within your web pages can cost you penalties in the search engines and also make your site look spammy and unprofessional.

There are numerous resources available on the web that can help with your keyword research. One very useful resource is the *Adwords Keyword Planner* provided by Google.

Adwords is Google's own PPC (Pay Per Click) advertising service and provides this tool to allow customers to research keywords to bid on. We can use this tool to get an idea of how many searches are conducted using our initial list of keywords, and refine our list to only include the most popular search terms and phrases. You can sign up for a free account by visiting http://adwords.google.com

If you follow the steps throughout this book you will insert your keywords into numerous strategic locations within your website to help it perform well in search engines when a user conducts a search using those terms. Taking some time to get this right from the start will pay significant dividends and put your business on the fast track to Internet success.

Choosing a Domain Name

A *domain name* (e.g. example.com) is a name used to identify a particular website on the internet. What this name actually represents is the numeric IP (Internet Protocol) address of a web server containing the actual files making up a website.

All devices on the internet connect to each other using these IP addresses. When you type a web address into a browser to visit a website, the browser automatically looks up the correct IP address for the server using DNS (a directory associating internet names with numbers) and seeks the web page from the web server located at the returned address.

You will need a domain name to identify your new website on the Internet. You can register these names via a domain registrar, in addition to most web hosting companies offering this as a service. After selecting a name you should use the registrars search service to verify it has not already been taken and is available to be registered by yourself.

When choosing a domain name think carefully about how relevant it is to your niche or business, how memorable it may be for people searching for your business or brand, and how complicated it may be for users to type into a web browser.

You should also try to include one or two of your *keywords* within your domain name (e.g. bobscarparts.com) but *do not* seek to register a domain name that *exactly* matches one of your main keyword phrases (e.g. usedcarparts.com). This once effective strategy was used to game search engines in the past, and in the case of competitive keywords, thanks to changes in search algorithms such as Google's *Exact Match Domain* update, could result in a penalty for your website.

After you have chosen, registered, and set-up a suitable domain name for your website, as directed by your web hosting provider, and once DNS servers have updated to reflect your new information, you are ready to go ahead and start creating the actual content for your site and uploading the pages that make up your website to your web server.

Creating your Web Pages

As mentioned previously a website is a collection of pages. These pages usually take the form of a text file that contains both text to be displayed, and special formatting information to display items in a particular way, and add functionality to the page, a clickable link or embedded image for example. This formatting, or mark-up uses an easy to learn language named *Hyper Text Mark-up Language* (HTML).

If you do not wish to learn all the ins and outs of HTML, you should at the very least make yourself familiar with it as many of the topics discussed in this manual do require some familiarity. Even if you choose to use some form of editor to create your web pages, for which there are many available, you should still endeavor to understand the concepts involved.

Some web hosting companies offer an online editor as part of your web hosting service. These can be an excellent place for a beginner to start creating full featured web pages with a minimum of knowledge. You can always use these editors to lay out your web pages in a visual manner, and then edit the page *source file* at a later time in order to implement the recommendations set out in this guide.

Planning your Web Pages

The first thing to consider when planning the pages for your website is the structure that your website will take. When a user types your domain name only (no file or path specified) into a browser, e.g. www.example.com, they will be shown the default *index page* for the website. This default page should be your starting point with all additional pages linked from here. This file is usually named *index.html* or *default.html* (or similar) and should be created in the top root directory of your website. Check with your web hosting provider for the correct *default filename* used on your web hosting platform as this varies from provider to provider.

You should define exactly what information you wish to appear on this main index page, and what other information you wish to include on one or more additional pages that you will create. A user on your site will navigate amongst these pages using a menu, navigation bar, or other links you add to your pages. A typical example of a basic business website structure might be something like;

- **Home** page (main Index) containing basic company info with links to additional pages:
- **About** page containing detailed company info.
- **Products** page(s) listing products for sale.
- **Contact** page listing location, phone number and email address.
- **Terms & Conditions** page showing your terms of business.
- **Privacy Policy** page stating how you use information obtained via your website and other privacy related issues.

You would obviously add (or remove) pages to fit your particular needs, but with the example above it would seem appropriate to create a menu or navigation bar with the following links:

Home – Products - About – Terms – Privacy - Contact

Each of these pages must be created individually and given unique filenames. In the case of the main index page (often called the home page) our file name is set for us, in most cases 'index.html', however the additional files you will create should be given meaningful names such as products.html, about.html, terms.html and so on. Also be sure to read the comments related to file names in the next section - *Search Engine Optimization*.

Once created and placed on your server, your web page can be accessed via the web using a combination of your domain name and the unique filename. In our example above we could access our products page directly by typing *www.example.com/products.html* into our browser. You would also make the word 'Products' in your menu or navigation into a hyper link, that when clicked upon, will move the users browser to that page.

Website Tracking & Analytics

It is important to track and monitor your website traffic using *web analytics* software that will log your visitor's movements throughout your site, providing valuable metrics and data. *Google Analytics* is a popular tracking platform offering a free service to website owners. Simply add a few supplied lines of code to the web page(s) you want to track, and then log-in to view your data, charts and other useful information.

Some web hosting providers also offer some form of tracking software as part of the service and so you should check with your web host as to availability and installation information.

Use analytic software and website statistics to learn what other sites and pages on the internet are driving traffic to your website, and which pages on your website are the most popular and best performing. You can also use your analytics to gauge the effectiveness of paid advertising campaigns by calculating your return on investment (ROI) for your ads.

Once armed with this vital marketing information you can seek to improve problem areas of your site and concentrate your efforts more efficiently on the website promotion activities that work well, dropping the less effective promotional channels. The same refinement can be performed with regards to our keywords, perhaps dropping those that do not produce sales and concentrating on those that do.

This constant process of analysis and modification of your website should be an *ongoing process* on a regular basis as trends change, pages go stale and a host of other reasons you should not take your eye off the ball.

Marketing a Website

Build it and they will come, it was said. The cold reality of marketing a website online is that without continuous efforts to promote your business website, using both online website marketing, and promotion in the real world, they will not come in the numbers required to make any business a success.

The first step in successfully promoting your website should be to devise a plan for your website marketing. Your online marketing plan would generally employ multiple channels, including; traditional advertising, and more importantly, search engine optimization of your web pages to achieve high rankings in search engine results for your related keywords.

Advertising internet services, or an online business, can be broken down into two main areas; website marketing online via the Internet, and marketing your website offline with traditional methods. Marketing a business on the internet takes two general forms, both of which should be considered as part of your overall *website marketing plan*;

- **FREE Advertising** - *Organic* search engine results, links from other websites, directories and social media marketing.

- **PAID Advertising** - Banner and text link adverts; rich media and featured (paid) search engine results.

When you first start to promote an online business, your site will be new to the web, and therefore new to search engines. It is unlikely that you would initially receive much traffic from organic channels so you may need to rely upon paid website advertising to start with. The aim, over time, is to also build a steady stream of low cost, or free organic traffic.

Free Internet Marketing

Everyone likes the word 'Free', and whilst in many aspects of life, and business, the phrase 'you get what you pay for' is a wise attitude, the same does not ring true for Internet marketing. Without a doubt, when done correctly, the *free* marketing resources available to you can yield far more results than costly paid advertising, and therefore the main focus of this book. This section takes a look at the resources available to your business with no cost.

Organic Search Engine Traffic

The number one *free* method of marketing an online business would have to be organic traffic from *Search Engine Result Pages* (SERPs). Most internet traffic originates from search results, and so tapping into this unlimited stream of targeted traffic should be made your priority.

If your website is listed within the first 3 pages of search results for related keyword(s) then you can look forward to a steady stream of free, targeted traffic for your website. Make it to the first page and the traffic flow increases with your position in the results.

Gaining a top position for related keyword(s) in the search engine results is usually obtained by tweaking a website to help search engines learn about the topic of your website and related keywords. This process of fine tuning a website can be performed with the use of *SEO* techniques, and can prove to be a very wise investment of time and resources, given the additional traffic it can yield. See the following section on *Search Engine Optimization* for details on fine tuning your website to obtain a better position in search engines.

Social Network Shares

The use of *Social Networking* can be a great way to promote your site. By using the power of *social media marketing* in your online business you can draw additional attention to your website, company, product or brand.

Harnessing the power of social media marketing via social networking sites such as Facebook, Google+, and Twitter is another vital ingredient for the success for any advertising or marketing campaign for your organization or business.

Social networks allow its users to share views, comments, and content. If you produce social content that users will want to share, it can create a small army of users pushing your brand awareness by sharing it with friends and contacts. Search engines are also looking closer at the social activity related to websites and play an ever increasing role as a ranking signal. See section on *Social Media Marketing*.

Natural Website Backlinks

A major ranking factor is *natural* links from other websites that point to pages on your site. When we say natural we mean links that are considered by the search engines to be *editorial votes* for the site in question.

Not all links are considered equal and major search engines will look at both the quality of the site linking to you, and its relevance to your topic or niche. This topic is covered in more detail later in this guide however as a general guide you should seek to obtain links *only* from related quality websites.

Create valuable, interesting and unique content for your users and they will want to link to it organically from other websites over time. The focus should be on providing creative and useful content for your readers, with the reward being free website backlinks!

Web Directory Sites

The value of a free listing in web directories has fallen in recent times, both in terms of link value for search engines and potential traffic from these lesser used resources; however a listing in a relevant niche directory can prove to be a valuable source of new potential customers and traffic to your site.

Only add your website to high quality directories, ideally within your own niche, making sure you select the correct category for your particular site. Ensure you list your site manually, using unique titles and description text for each submission, and only submit your website or blog *once*.

Don't use automated submission software to submit your pages to hundreds of directories as this is often detected (because the titles and descriptions will all be the same), and considered as *spam* by major search engines. Secondly many of these links are of *low quality and relevance* meaning such links could actually have a negative, instead of positive, impact on your rankings.

Paid Internet Marketing

The following *paid* advertising services should also be considered as part of your website marketing plan, and can, depending upon your business, yield amazing results. When trying out these services, use a limited budget and use your tracking software to monitor your advertising campaigns closely to quickly identify what works, and adjusting your promotion campaigns accordingly. As it can take a number of weeks for search engines to spider and list your website, you might like to use a paid service to give your website an initial boost until your website is receiving a steady flow of free organic traffic from search engines.

Paid Search Engine Listings

Most of the major search engines allow you to purchase a prime placement within the search results pages, quite often located above the standard organic results. This ad space is sold usually on a CPC (cost per click) model, via a bid for keywords type system.

Google Adwords are the largest provider, with Bidvertiser coming in a distant second. Facebook also offers a similar service. This type of advertising provides a cost effective additional stream of traffic to your website within a controlled campaign budget.

Target your ad campaign effectively by using your keywords to ensure your ad appears in relevant searches for your product or nice.

Banner Advertising

Banner advertising is another good form of internet promotion online, providing cost per click (CPC), or a cost per 1000 displays (CPM) advertising model.

An advertising *banner* usually consists of an image, or text area, devoted to advertising your product or service, whereby the user will be transported to your site when they click on the ad.

Banner ads are available in a wide range of possible sizes and you should try a good variation for best results. Using your tracking software, along with the information provided by the banner supplier, fine tune your ad campaigns to use the most effective and best performing banner types and sizes.

In addition to Google Adwords banner advertising offerings, it is also worth considering the use of Bidvertiser to increase your overall advertising exposure.

Section Summary

- You need *web space* for your website files, from a reliable **Web Hosting** provider.
- You need to research your target **Keywords** and phrases for your niche or market.
- You need a **Domain Name** (*example.com*) that ideally contains one or two target keywords.
- You need to construct and market a **Search Engine Friendly** website, optimized for your keywords.

SECTION 2 – WEBSITE SEO

What is SEO?

SEO - *Search Engine Optimization* is the term given to obtaining traffic for your website from "organic" free listings in search engine result pages (SERPS). Google, Yahoo and Bing all show these pages when a user enters a search term or phrase into a search box located on one of these search engines. The key to search optimization, and tapping into this free traffic, is to get your website listed as high as possible in these search pages for keyword(s) related to your company or business.

2013 and 2014 were interesting years with regards to search optimization. A range of updates from major search engines signaled a new dawn, where simply pointing thousands of unrelated links, using keywords as anchor text, at a website to make it rank on the first page of results not only met an abrupt end, but could also get your website penalized, or worse still, removed from the index altogether.

Now, more than ever, on-page search optimization is critical to obtaining high search rankings, alongside quality content and the end-user experience.

The resources in this section will help you achieve better search results by walking you through various sections and aspects of your website design that may require some modification in order to achieve better search engine results, all without the risk of sanctions or other penalties for using techniques frowned upon my the major search engines.

Effective search engine optimization involves several different fundamental tasks and concepts, namely;

- Optimizing your web content to be search engine friendly.

- Creating unique and compelling content for your users.

- Enhancing your user experience, including page load times.

- Employ Social Media Marketing to boost your brand.

- Links to your website (quality and relevance over quantity).

Within this section we mainly discuss the most important aspects related to website design and content optimization; however the other points above will be addressed briefly towards the end of the chapter.

Search Optimize Website Content

Search engine optimization is most effective when you create unique, quality, compelling content for your website that also contains your related keywords. When you adopt this strategy you not only boost your rankings but provide more value for your website visitors.

If you create great quality content other people will want to link to it, either from relevant websites or related blogs, or by sharing it on social networks. This provides a stream of free traffic, in addition to sending search engines all the right signals.

The purpose of this section is to provide a quick and easy guide to help you when creating or editing your website to make it perform well in search engines and promote a steady stream of traffic to your website.

Explaining each of the items in depth and how it relates to search engine algorithms is beyond the scope of this book, we concentrate strictly upon the vital information you need to know and how it should be implemented on your own website for maximum performance.

Changes you make to your website can take some time to be updated by search engines, sometimes running into weeks. Be patient and wait for search engines to crawl through your site, obtain the updated information and index it correctly within its database(s).

Run through the SEO checklist in this section, in the order shown, to achieve the best search rankings for your website.

1. Page Title Tags

The HTML *title* tag is used within your page source code to assign a title to each individual page on your website. These tags provide information that is used by a web browser to display the page title, usually in the browsers main title bar, or alternatively within the tab in the case of a tabbed browser.

Search engines also use the information within your title to help classify your page, often using it as the clickable text part of your entry when your page is displayed in search engine results.

The contents of your title tag for each page plays a major role with regards to search engine ranking. Optimizing these tags for search will give you a boost in rankings on its own and so should not be overlooked. Optimize the title tags for each of your web pages, as described below, before moving on to other items in this checklist.

Create unique title tags for each page on your site. Each page on your site should have its own distinct title that is unique throughout your site.

Use brief, but descriptive titles that accurately describe the page's content. Include your keywords first, and then your site name, as shown in the examples below:

Examples:

    <title>keyword1 keyword2 keyword3 - sitename</title>

    <title>1992 MX5 Wing Mirror – Bobs Car Parts</title>

The title tag should be placed within the *head* section of your page, between the opening *<head>* and closing *</head>* tags as shown below;

<html>
<head>
<title>Example Page Title</title>
</head>
<body>
...
<!-- main content →
...
</body>
</html>

Use 70 characters or less for your title tags as longer titles will be truncated by search engines in most cases. It is important to include relevant keywords for the page, but do not repeat keywords more than twice within a page title.

Refrain from the use of all uppercase characters within your page title and avoid the use of strange or unusual symbols.

Remember to make sure each page title is unique within the scope of your website, duplicated page titles are confusing for the user, and frowned upon by search engines. Each unique title should contain targeted keywords that are relevant to the contents of the page.

Search engines index web pages, not websites, and so each individual page title should target *different* keyword combinations.

2. Description Meta Tag

Each individual web page should have a HTML *meta-description* tag, again located within the *<head>* section of your page, describing the actual content contained on the page. This description text is often used in search engine result pages (SERPs) to describe the page within results, and usually shown beneath your page title in search listings. Grabbing a users attention here is vital, so be sure to include a call to action.

You should ensure that all your web pages have unique, relevant and search optimized meta-description tags before moving on to the next item in this checklist.

Example:

<meta name="description" content="Click to buy MX5 wings mirrors and other great parts via our online store. Huge discounts at Bobs parts!">

The description tag should be placed within the head section of your page, i.e. between the <head> and </head> tags as shown in the example below;

<html>
<head>
<title>Example Page Title</title>
<meta name="description" content="Example Description">
</head>
<body>
...
</body>
</html>

Try to make your page descriptions engaging to the end user as well as optimizing for search engines. Remember that this, combined with your page title, is often the first thing a user sees of your website, listed amongst other similar listings, so make it stand out from the crowd!

Use less than 160 standard characters for your page description, and again try to integrate your targeted keywords. Try not to repeat your keywords too often and ensure it would make sense to a human reader who is less likely to click through to a site with a nonsense description.

Finally, remember to include a well crafted *call to action* or something to entice a user to click through to your website.

3. Optimized Page URLs

As you know, the individual pages and resources on your (or any other) website are accessed via a *Uniform Resource Locator* (URL), e.g. *http://www.yoursite.com/index.html*. The structure of your web page URLs is an important factor for both human and search engine alike. Try to structure your directory paths and web page filenames to reflect the content of the web page, keeping them simple and short, while embedding some of your related targeted keywords.

Example: Optimized static page URL;

www.bobsparts.com/mx5-1999-mirror.html

Example: Optimized directory URL;

www.bobsparts.com/mx5/1999/mirror/

Shorter URLs tend to perform better than longer ones so keep them short and relevant, while at the same time including your required keywords. URLs should be all lower case, and so should your filenames. Use a hyphen (-) character as a separator between your keywords and avoid using other special symbols in your URLs.

Also ensure that your URL will make sense to a human reader, while including relevant keywords for the page. As with previous items covered so far, search engines also use the information embedded in your URLs to help classify the topic of the page, or group of pages within a directory, and so you should optimize your URLs before moving on further with your SEO tasks.

4. Site Navigation

Good navigation of your website is important in helping your visitors quickly find what they want. It can also help search engines understand what content is important to your website.

Your website navigation should be easy to understand and based on a hierarchy, starting at your home (root) page. Try to group similar items in a tree like formation, ideally with no page any further than 3 clicks away from your home page.

There is some evidence to suggest that text links are given more weight as a ranking factor than image links and so it stands to reason that the same would apply to links within your website navigation.

Use text links to create your menu(s) and use relevant keywords associated with the target page as the anchor text as opposed to generic terms like 'Home'.

Again, it is important to strike a balance here between using search engine optimized text, while still providing a quality experience for your website end user.

Search engines are not very good at reading *JavaScript*, and cannot understand *Java Applets* or *Flash* components. While it cannot be disputed that these technologies bring a new dimension to web pages, they do not suit our purposes with regard to fine tuning of our website for search engines.

Given the weight placed upon navigation as a ranking factor, we would suggest you avoid the use of these (and similar) technologies in respect of your website navigation. Use cascading style scripts (CSS) to create nice looking but search engine friendly menus and navigation.

It would seem that at least one major search engine frown a little upon suicidal links, that is to say, links on a page that link to the same page, calling itself and going nowhere new.

This small quality flag is often triggered inadvertently by webmasters that copy a block of code containing the website navigation to all pages on the website.

All seems fine at first glance, but you will have added a link to some of your pages that link to the page in question. For example, your contact page may well contain a link in its own navigation bar to the contact page, causing confusion when a user clicks the link which simply reloads the same page. Disable these suicidal links by removing the anchor tags that surround the clickable text, or by removing the link altogether.

Finally, website navigation does not need to be located in one place. Many websites opt for placing the most important pages in a navigation area toward the top of the page, with pages of lesser importance, such as links to your privacy policy, contact page etc., placed in a footer located at the bottom of the page.

Search engines tend to value the content that is located towards the top of the page over content located lower down, and so this split navigation style would make sense for improved SEO.

5. Unique Quality Content

Nobody likes a copy-cat, and the major search engines are no different. Unique content is favored over scraped or spun content, which can get your site penalized. Moreover, users know good content when they see it, and will naturally share your hard work by creating a buzz on social networks, forums and similar online communities if you deliver.

The days where content is king are over. Purchasing a bunch of articles from another website, slapping them up on the web and pointing a bunch of links at the site, will no longer suffice with the latest search engine algorithms. In fact the results of such actions will probably be counter-productive.

Only publish *unique content* that you have created yourself, ensuring high quality with regards to content, grammar, spelling and accuracy.

When pushed on the point of *what makes a quality website*, the head of Google's web spam team stated that to qualify a web page should bring something new to the web. Filling your web page with nothing but content obtained from other websites will not be enough to achieve high rankings, you must add some value of your own in some way.

Search engines seem to also favor content that is updated often, tending to index blog sites more often, but this is not always the case.

Some content is simply timeless and is not expected to change often. Other, more time sensitive content is more likely to be pushed down in the rankings by more up to date information.

Your keywords should appear within your content several times, spread evenly throughout the page, starting with your most important and working them into the text in a natural sounding way.

You should also try to add variations of your keywords (synonyms) where possible, for maximum exposure.

Search engines pay particularly close attention to highlighted words in bold or italics contained within a web page, and are a *strong* ranking factor.

Emphasize each of your main keywords *ONCE* within your main content text, using bold formatting, via the <b> or <strong> tags, and then *ONCE* again, this time in italics using the <i> or <em> HTML tags.

Example:

This is a <b>keyword</b> in bold, but this <i>keyword</i> is shown in italics.

Another excellent way to add new fresh content to your website on a regular basis is to add a *Blog* (web log) to your site. Posting regular blog post entries will gain the search engines attention with new content, at the same time as increasing how often your website is crawled and indexed.

A blog also offers the opportunity to interact with your customers on a more personal level, gaining further valuable insights into your customers needs, and providing a human face to your brand or business.

6. Optimized Anchor Text

The text you use to link to other pages, the *anchor text*, plays an important role for SEO, and achieving good rankings. When linking to other pages on your own site, try to use text links over images, and use keyword rich text that describes the page you are linking to. Try to avoid the use of generic anchor text such as 'click here', 'more' or 'home' etc.

While conducting Search Engine Optimization strategies such as SEO Link Building, it is easy for some webmasters to lose sight of how they use anchor text and the HTML anchor tag on their own website or blog.

Internal links, those pointing to URLs on your own website, and external linking, where you link to pages on other websites, are treated very differently by search engines. Here we discuss both types of linking strategies to help you get your SEO and Links working together to improve your search rankings.

The use of text linking instead of images and buttons is the best choice as search engines seem to favor these types of links and give them more weight as a ranking factor. For this reason you should try to use text linking wherever possible, especially when linking to internal pages on your website.

Avoid the use of generic terms and phrases such as 'Home', 'Click Here', 'More' etc. Unless you wish to rank for these terms they serve little purpose with regards to SEO. You should strive to use related keywords within your anchor text, both for internal and external linking, both of which are described in more detail below.

HTML Code for a Hyperlink

The HTML code for a *hyperlink* uses an *anchor tag* to make elements of your page clickable and open another URL when clicked by a user. A basic example showing the elements related to SEO is shown below.

Anchor Tag Format

    `<a href="`*URL*`" target="`*TARGET*`">LINK TEXT</a>`

URL - The full URL to the resource or page to open.

TARGET - Location to open the URL. Can be any of the following values;

   _blank - opens a new un-named browser window
   _parent - opens in parent frame or window
   _self - replaces current frame or browser window
   _top - loads in top frame
   framename - a named frame or browser window

Omitting the *target* value will cause the link to open in the current window or frame.

LINK TEXT - This is the actual clickable text that is displayed on your page, or alternatively an image tag in order to display an image that you want to make into a clickable link. The keywords you should try to use are those related to the target page you are linking to, not the current page.

Example:

<a href="http://www.ezwebsitepromotion.com" target="_blank">Website Promotion</a>

The example shown above will open our website located at *www.ezwebsitepromotion.com* in a *new* browser window, when the text *'Website Promotion'* is clicked.

Internal Anchor Text Linking

Anchor text for *internal* linking should always contain keywords related to the target page. Linking text containing two to three words seems to work best. Follow the same strategy for your website menu and site navigation links.

Only use related and relevant keywords that appear on the target page as opposed to the page containing the link. Try to avoid linking to the same page more than two or three times from the same web page, as this can look spammy to search engines.

External Anchor Text Linking

SEO link building to external websites is still a relevant factor for your own website as search engines also look at the sites that you link out to when ranking your website. Again use relevant anchor text only.

We have seen some success in linking outward to other quality sites using our targeted keywords, but only link to well established, trusted, authority sites.

Linking to bad or unrelated websites can cost you ranking positions and in severe cases, such as linking to hacking websites etc., can get your site banned (sand-boxed).

It is also a good idea when external linking, to open the URL in a new browser window to ensure you do not lose your user if they click the link. Use the Target value of the anchor tag to specify "_*blank*" as the target for the new page.

Links pointing to a web page are seen by search engines as virtual votes for the page in question. Each web page on a website holds a Google assigned value, often referred to as *link juice* that is passed on to pages that you link to. This value is derived largely from the number and quality of links pointing to the page, and the value Google assigned those pages.

This ranking factor essentially places a numeric value on your virtual vote for another page. Link juice is divided amongst all of the links on a page, both internal and external, equally. For this reason it is a good idea to restrict the number of out-going links on a page in order to avoid the value passed to your own internal pages from being diluted.

7. SEO & Images

Whilst major search engines cannot make much sense of the content of an actual image, they do however try to make sense of the information contained within the images *<img>* HTML tag, notably the text contained within the *alt* parameter and the *filename* given to the actual image file.

Example:

<img src="[image file]" alt="[description text]">

Search engine crawlers will read the alt parameter of your <img> tags in order to understand what the image represents. You should include your keywords, especially with linked images, while trying to describe the image. A good strategy is to consider what you would likely use as anchor text for a standard text link and use that information for your image's alt parameter.

Try not to repeat the same keywords within a single alt tag and avoid duplicate alt tags on an individual page. Use unique text in your alt tags for all images but keep them limited to 3 or 4 keywords related to the containing page, however, it is important to remember, as with text links above, the keywords chosen should be appropriate for the target page if the image is used as a link.

Alt Parameter Example;

<img src="..." alt="MX5 Wing Mirror">

Follow the same procedures for optimizing your image file names, separating individual keywords with the '-' separator where needed.

Filename Example;

<img src="mx5-mirror-blue.gif" alt="...">

There does seem to be some weight placed on the displayed *location* of images, with those shown at the top of a page given more SEO clout. Therefore, images containing your most relevant keywords should appear towards the top of the page, with images containing lesser value keywords following underneath.

With website performance becoming an established ranking factor it is also important to look at the number of images contained within a single page. Page load speed will be negatively affected by a large number of images, and in turn may have a negative impact on your site rankings. Keep to a reasonable number of images on a single page and ensure each image file has been optimized (compressed) for use on the web to obtain the smallest possible file sizes.

Avoid the use of very small images (e.g. 1x1 pixel image) and small transparent images as a means to inject more links or text (via alt tags) as this is seen as spammy by most major search engines and could cost you in your fight for higher rankings.

It should also be noted that a page full of images, but containing little or no relevant text, will not be considered of value to the end user, and therefore unlikely to rank well.

8. Use of Heading Tags

HTML *Heading* tags are used to structure the information on a web page to aid users find the information they are looking for. Search engines also use them in a similar way to help decide the topic or relevance of your page.

There are six sizes/types of heading tag, starting with the *<h1>* tag, the most significant, and ending with the *<h6>* tag, the least important.

Heading tags typically make text contained within them larger than normal on the page, a visual clue to users that this text is important and could help them understand about the type of content located beneath the heading.

Multiple heading sizes are used to create a hierarchical structure for your content, making it easier to navigate through your document.

Example;

...
<h1>1999 MX5 Parts</h1>
<h2>Near Side Wing Mirror</h2>
Here we have a near side wing mirror for a 1999 MX5.
<h3>Price</h3>
New: 99.99 Used: 49.99
<h2>More MX5 Miata Used Car Parts</h2>
...

As you might expect, search engines give weight to these tags on a sliding scale, with the *h1* and *h2* tags given the most weight. You should concentrate your main efforts within these two tags, ideally placed towards the top of the page.

Try to implement your main keywords for the page, where suitable, within your heading tags, with your main keywords embedded in the *h1* tag, secondary keywords in your *h2* tag etc.

Only use a *single* h1 tag per individual page as search engines may consider this spam. You can use the other heading tags multiple times, in moderation, keeping the page readable for the user, and keeping them within the context of the page contents.

Remember these headings tags must also be readable using natural language and make sense to the human visitors of your website.

9. Other Page Content

This section may appear late in this checklist, but each of the previous areas of website content optimization covered so far require the presence of unique quality content on each of your web pages, and this content should also be optimized for search engines.

Content length is a factor that should not be ignored. On the one hand, a page with too much content may suffer from a search engine failing to index the entire page in addition to slow loading times and the potential penalty that follows. On the other hand, a page with little content is unlikely to be seen of as offering value to users of the internet. Your content should be at least 500 - 800 words and contain your keywords spread sparingly throughout the text.

Try to mention each keyword or phrase several times throughout your text, starting with your main keyword. For each instance of a specific keyword you should have one instance *bolded* (using the <b> or <strong> tags), with another instance of the keyword shown in *italics* (using the <i> or <em> tags), with at least one other instance shown in normal text. Use the same procedure with your secondary keywords. It is also a good idea to ensure some of these tagged keywords appear towards the top of the page layout.

Avoid the overuse of keywords within your text; ensuring additional relevant text is present, including alternative words for your keywords. If the ratio of keywords on your page is too high this can be seen as 'keyword stuffing' and cost you a spam penalty. If your page does not make sense to a human reader then it is likely your have overused your keywords.

Text located towards the top of the page seems to have more traction. Ensure each of your keywords is shown at least once *above the fold* (the area at the top of a web page visible to a user without being required to scroll the page).

The quality of your website in the eyes of major search providers may be judged based upon the experience you offer your users. Is your site easy to navigate? Supported on different browsers? Fast loading pages? Free of viruses or other malicious code? Contains quality, unique content?

Ensure the quality of your content with regards to spelling and grammar. These types of errors can cost you dearly, for example a badly spelled keyword will not help you rank for the correctly spelled version, and could raise quality flags against your site.

Proof read all of your content to ensure it is easy to read and understand. Perform a *spell check* on all of your web pages and correct any errors you find. The same rule applies to all titles, headings and descriptions for your site.

10. Create a Blog

Creating a blog (web log) for your website or business can offer numerous benefits, both to your customers, and in terms of SEO. An increase in rankings has been seen for sites where a blog has been added, and properly linked to from the main website, using the main domain of the site.

Example; *http://blog.domain.com*

To get the maximum benefit from your blog, first create at least 8 quality blog posts, containing at least 500 words each, and then keep posting on a regular basis to prevent your blog going stale. Optimize your blog pages using the same SEO methods as outlined in this checklist.

Search engines love blogs and you'll often see a stream of new traffic, if you remember to link back to your main site from your blog pages! Blog posts are an excellent place to insert more keywords into the mix, and if you create quality articles of value to your users you will be enticing them to share your content on other blogs and social networking platforms.

The creation of your own blog will also allow you to communicate with your visitors, leads and customers in a more conversational manner, leading to valuable feedback and insight into your customer's needs and current trends. Always use a friendly tone in your blog posts, avoiding hard sales and marketing statements, while encouraging your users to share, interact and participate in discussions related to the content of your articles, as these social interactions are serving an increasing role as a ranking factor in SEO.

11. Search Engine Crawlers

You may not want certain pages of your website crawled and indexed because they might not be useful to users if found in a search engine's results, or from an SEO stand-point, are not relevant to the topic(s) that make up the rest of your site (a contact or privacy policy page for example is unlikely to be relevant to your chosen topic/keywords). Search engines can be instructed to ignore pages, and not follow certain links. This can be achieved in two ways:

a) Robots Meta Tag

You can add a *robots meta tag* to any page on your website and it may contain any combination of the following values in a comma separated list;

NOINDEX, NOFOLLOW and *NOARCHIVE*

NOINDEX will prevent the page from being indexed (listed) by search engines.

NOFOLLOW will prevent the links on the page being followed by the crawler.

NOARCHIVE prevents the search engine from caching a copy of the current page.

Example;

<meta name="robots" content="NOINDEX,NOFOLLOW"/>

In the above example the page containing this tag would not be indexed, and the links contained within it would not be followed.

b) Robots.txt File

A *robots.txt* file is a plain text file that tells search engines whether they can access parts of your site. This file must be named "robots.txt" and be placed within the root directory of your website.

This file uses the *Robots Exclusion Protocol* to specify the parts of the site that may be accessed by the crawler. In the example below all resources except for those stored in the images folder are accessible.

Example;

*User-agent: ***
Disallow: /images/

Warning: Care should be taken when employing any of the above methods to restrict access to your web pages by search engine crawlers. Spending hours optimizing your titles and tweaking your text will not help if you have inadvertently instructed search engines to ignore an optimized page!

12. Using Sitemaps

While our thoughts are turned to how we can restrict pages of our site appearing in search engines, it is worth giving equal consideration to ensuring that search engines can in fact access and index all the pages we have worked so hard to optimize!

We can do this effectively by using a number of free *sitemap generators* to scan our completed website and create a special XML file called a *sitemap*, containing a list of links that we want to be crawled and indexed.

Once created, this sitemap can then be submitted to the search engines via your webmaster tools area to aid them in discovering the links or your site and indexing them properly.

You can also notify search engines about the existence of your sitemap from within your *robots.txt* file.

Example;

User-agent: *
Disallow: /images/
...
Sitemap: http://www.yoursite.com/sitemap.xml

It can also be worthwhile for your visitors and search engines alike to create a *human readable* sitemap, that is to say, create a page containing a well structured list of links to all of the pages on your website.

13. Setting Correct Language

The HTML *lang* attribute can be used to declare the language of a Web page using ISO Language Codes. This is meant to assist search engines and browsers identify the language used for the content of that particular page.

Making sure that search engines correctly identify the language of a page is beneficial to both users and your SEO efforts, especially if your pages are not written in English and you want a boost in those language orientated listings.

For a **HTML** page you should declare the primary language for each Web page using the *lang* attribute of the *<html>* tag, for example:

*<html **lang="en"**>*

...
</html>

In **XHTML**, the language of the page is also declared from within the *<html>* tag, in two locations as show below:

*<html xmlns="http://www.w3.org/1999/xhtml" **lang="en"** **xml:lang="en"**>*

...
</html>

An appropriate setting for the *lang* attribute is any valid ISO 639-1 Language Code. See **Appendix B** for a complete list of countries and associated ISO Language Codes.

SECTION 3 - VIDEO SEO

Introduction to Video SEO

Video SEO optimization and promotion is a new and exciting form of internet marketing, and a way to increase your overall brand exposure to new internet users that may otherwise have not been familiar with your product or brand. It is a great way to promote your website or business and will get you increased results with search engines.

Video search optimization is essential for successful indexing and ranking of your videos by search engines, and If you are just getting started with video marketing you will find these tips for optimizing web videos for Google and Youtube essential reading.

If you aren't optimizing your videos to match the common search terms used by people when searching the internet, your videos are likely to get lost among a huge number of alternative search listings and not reach their intended audience.

Youtube is currently the second largest search engine behind Google. A recent study suggested that Youtube videos are up to 50 times more likely to rank on the first page of Google search result pages. Video marketing is therefore a powerful medium for driving additional traffic to your website and increasing your brand awareness.

How do you take advantage of this online website promotion medium and ensure your videos get the desired results? With the use of video search engine optimization, often referred to as Video SEO.

Optimizing Videos

Use the following tips to help get your video on to the first page of Google and Youtube search results, but more importantly, tap into a large niche market that is interested in your products or services.

1. Video Content

Try to keep the content of your marketing videos relevant, informative, and rich in useful content that is related to your particular brand or product(s).

Informative videos containing step-by-step instructions and videos expressing opinions about relevant topics can be popular, keeping in mind that videos should always be fun, informative, and memorable, leaving a lasting impression with the viewer wanting to know and see more.

In the same way that web page quality issues can affect web page rankings, the same applies to video rankings. Video content should be of a high enough quality, provide some form of added value, and be unique in order to avoid duplicate content penalties.

2. Choosing Video Titles

Video *titles* are a strong ranking factor; in a similar way to title tags are on web pages. Catch the viewer's attention with a punchy video title that also contains your keyword phrases for your brand or service.

Do some keyword research to find the words and phrases that your target audience will most likely be searching for, but keep it interesting, and avoid the overuse of your keywords. Remember your video title must appeal to real people and search engines alike.

3. Video Description

An optimized *video description* is another strong factor with regards to the ranking of video content. Optimize your video's description using your relevant keywords to allow search engines to index and rank it higher and to help users better understand your video content. It is also a good place to engage your viewers with a call to action.

You can usually use quite a few words to describe your video and should not be afraid of using as much of this page real estate as possible. Go ahead and go as far as adding a transcript for your video here, if room allows, or add additional product information or sales copy.

Top Tip: Add your full website URL as the first line of your video description, followed by some relevant text. This is a valuable back link in terms of SEO and will help with your overall website rankings.

4. Choosing Tags

Optimize your video *Tags* using your important keyword phrases or individual keywords. Try to avoid the use of complicated and uncommon words or terminology in your video tags. Look at your keyword research and identify what your targeted audience is likely to use while searching to find your product, brand or service online.

Also consider renaming the actual video file using these keyword(s), in the same way as you would when optimizing image files, prior to uploading your video.

5. Video Transcripts

Provide transcripts of your online videos where possible, within reasonable size limits of course. Standard HTML text content is still a favorite source of information for search engines.

For your videos to rank well you need to give search engines something to read, index and rank. Surround your videos with relevant text that can be easily read and indexed by search engines. Providing a transcript not only supplies this relevant content but also offers an additional benefit to your viewers.

6. Video Length

For best SEO performance keep your video length to five minutes or less. The average amount of time a user spends watching a Youtube video is around 1 and a half minutes. If you have video(s) of long duration, consider breaking them up into smaller parts, and title/tag each to be more appealing to the viewer. Multiple videos are also better for your Video SEO optimization efforts.

Youtube is now paying closer attention to its viewers and users engagement with videos and so it is increasingly important that users watch your video for as long as possible, ideally to the end. Limiting your video length increases the chances of your video being viewed in its entirety.

SECTION 4 - SOCIAL MEDIA MARKETING

What is Social Media Marketing?

Social media marketing is a term used to describe the process of boosting website traffic, or brand awareness, through the use of social media networking sites.

Most social media marketing programs usually revolve around creating unique content that attracts attention and encourages the viewer to share it with their friends and contacts on social networks. Your business message spreads from one user to another and impacts with the user in a stronger way because it appears to originate from a trusted source, as opposed to the brand, business or company itself.

This type of powerful website marketing online is driven by word-of-mouth, resulting in earned exposure rather than paid advertisements. Social networking platforms tend to be easily accessible to anyone with internet access via a range of desktop and mobile devices.

So how big is this platform? At last count, Over 550 million Facebook users, 65 million tweets sent on twitter a day, 2 billion Youtube video views per day, and 1 billion page views per month for Tumblr. These numbers will only continue to grow as social media networking becomes more of the norm for everyday life.

Social Networking Benefits

Some benefits of *social networking* include; increased communication for business or other organizations, improved brand awareness, and often improves customer service and support. Additionally, social networking serves as a low cost platform for organizations to implement online marketing campaigns.

Social signals in SEO are playing an increasing role with major search engine rankings and social networking is certainly here to stay.

In addition to creating great content to encourage social shares, you should consider setting up your own business pages for your business with the top social networking sites and linking out to your new social pages from your website. Don't forget to also include a link back to your website on your social pages.

Encourage social sharing of your content by adding *'Like'* boxes to your web page content. We call them like boxes here but social networks often have a specific term for voting/sharing a piece of content, Facebook uses Like buttons whereas twitter has a tweet box and Google+ has a Plus 1 button. All these perform much the same task of sharing a particular piece of content on the appropriate social network.

You can obtain the HTML code required for these boxes and buttons via the appropriate social networks website. There are also a number of services available that allow you to quickly add a selection from various social networks with a single snippet of code.

Social Networking Sites

Blogs – Short for web-log. Locations on the web to log opinions, information, thoughts, or anything else you want to say on behalf of yourself, organization or business. Typically more casual and conversational in tone in order to encourage comments and feedback from readers. Our Internet Marketing blog is a good example (blog.ezwebsitepromotion.com), and contains many more online marketing tips and tricks.

Microblogs – This type of blog limits the number of letters or characters you can use in a single post. The most popular, Twitter, is used frequently to post quick thoughts or to share links to other useful information.

Social Network – These networks allow people to come together in an online community. The most popular sites would be Facebook, Google+ and LinkedIn (a business orientated social network).

Discussion Forum – Forums, perhaps the earliest type of social media, remains very popular today. People can come together in an online community and discuss specific topics.

Wikis – Websites that permit users to contribute directly to the actual content, such as Wikipedia, are known as wikis. They promote a community effort to provide the most accurate information possible by collectively contributing to one website or document.

Content Specific – Most commonly used for music, photo or video sharing, e.g. Pinterest, Flickr or Youtube. They promote online networking through a specific type of web content.

How to use Social Media

Social media plays a central role of many people's everyday lives and continues to grow. Today, this ever-evolving medium has moved past being merely a way to interact with people and has become an essential part of online marketing strategies for organizations and businesses of all types and sizes.

As a small business or company, leveraging the power of social networking can help you build relationships, understand new market and consumer demands and use social media content to influence and entice your target market.

Some top techniques used by those companies and organizations that are using social media and leveraging it to their advantage include:

Be conversational – Don't take your business too seriously on social media, this will quickly turn people away. Interact as if you are chatting with a potential customer. You should ask the customer questions, and engage in conversation rather than pushing your message on them. By doing this on social media sites you will see more long term success with your marketing campaigns.

Use a call to action – Some areas of marketing never change and a call to action is one of them. You still need to ask them to visit your website, or purchase a product via social media. But instead of using bright buttons as you would on a web page, or the common roadside signs, you use images and text to pass on to your customer what it is that you want them to do.

Provide something of value – Provide your visitors and customers with a reason to interact with you on social network sites by providing them with something they will consider of value. This could be quality content via blogs, or an exclusive discount for being loyal to your product or brand. Whatever you provide, make it something that your customers will appreciate.

Make it a two way street – People don't like to be 'talked at' on social networking sites, they use these networks as a way to engage. Real conversations are a two-way street, and no different with social media engagement. Interact with your users and you will soon get to know their wants and needs, and you may well discover a new niche you never knew existed.

Social Media Integration

Integrating social media marketing into your online promotion efforts can seem a daunting task as first. In the first instance we would suggest you follow the steps below as a starting point, and then build other channels as you become more comfortable with marketing within a social media context.

Facebook Page – Create a 'Like' page or dedicated account on Facebook for your business or organization. Link to, and promote your Facebook page from your own website. Make regular conversational posts and engage with your followers in a fun and friendly manner.

Twitter – Create a Twitter account for your business, and again promote your Twitter page via your website. Make regular posts and interact with others. Use hash tags to highlight keywords within your posts by appending the pound symbol ('#'), e.g. #MX5 car parts sale all day. Hash tags are now also supported by Facebook.

Create a Blog – Creating a Blog is a great way to keep customers up to date with new information, and search engines love them. For your blog to be taken seriously by search engines you must post at least 8 quality blog posts as soon as you can and then continue to post on a regular basis. In my case I use a blog to post SEO tips that either didn't make it into this book, or did not warrant inclusion our main website. Ideally create a sub-domain on your website for your blog pages, e.g. *blog.yoursite.com*

Video Marketing – Create your own Youtube channel and upload/embed instructional or promotional videos within your website. Use the Video SEO strategies laid out in Part 3 VIDEO SEO.

Shown above are just a few suggestions on where to start your online social media marketing efforts and reflects both size and quality of the social networks, in addition to those of benefit in regards to Search Engine Optimization.

Linking to your own website from many of these well established authority sites will help your site achieve higher search rankings and makes a good start for any link building campaign.

The installation of visitor tracking software on your website, if you have not already done so, can be of great benefit when it comes to keeping an eye on the effectiveness of your online social network marketing campaign.

Top Tip

It pays to keep your eye on your reports with regards to which social media networking efforts actually pay off in terms of website traffic. Things can change quickly on the internet and so you should adjust your efforts accordingly. As we enter 2015 our own social media efforts will be placed not on Twitter, Youtube, or even Facebook, but on a rapidly growing site called Pinterest.com. This website alone yields our sites more social traffic than the other three put together.

This may well be the case for you too, so sign up for a free *Pinterest* account and start following users, who in most cases will follow you back. Next, search the site for relevant images for your topic, and *Repin*. View the Pin on your own board and click Edit. Change the current URL to one of your choosing and click Save. When this Pin is shared (repined) it will now carry your link along with it. Easy traffic!

...N 5 - OFF-PAGE OPTIMIZATION

Off-Page SEO

Most of the tasks previously outlined in this book relate to SEO factors located within your web pages. There are also a number of off-page activities that are essential for the on-going success of your website.

Links to your Website

While conducting website marketing online, you may see many references to *back links*, a link located on another external website that points to a page on your own website. These links back to your website are seen by search engines as an editorial vote in favor of your website and as such considered a major external ranking factor. Building a good portfolio of quality website back links is essential to the success of any website and should make up a significant proportion of your SEO activities.

There may have been a time when buying thousands of bad quality links to your site would propel you to the top of the search listings. After several updates by Google it is now the fastest way to get your website punished, or perhaps even removed from the index altogether!

So is the use of back links for SEO dead? No. But now Google pays far more attention to quality, editorial links, than it does to spam blog comments and forum posts. In fact inbound links from some blog networks could get you banned from search engines and leave you with a huge link cleanup operation to undertake.

Back Link Quality

The total number of links pointing to any web page used to be a major ranking signal. These days it is fair to say that all links are not created equal and that SEO link building is now very much about link quality over quantity.

Major search engines look at the quality of the links pointing at your website as well as the number. Try to avoid using automated submission software and other similar link building tools as the use of such techniques could get your site banned, or at the very least your rankings penalized. We have reached page one for a website with less than 20 links, it really is about quality over quantity.

Do not buy links, as paid links for the purposes of gaming search engines is a breach of webmaster terms for major search providers.

Do not participate in any link exchange networks or similar artificial link building techniques as part of your website optimization strategy. Instead, concentrate on obtaining quality editorial links from established authority sites, within your niche, by creating great value and compelling content that other website owners and webmasters will want to link to and share on social networks.

Link Density & Diversity

Recent updates have penalized websites for the excessive use of keywords in anchor text for incoming links. Natural links, those created by other webmasters because they like your content, would not all link using the same anchor/link text and nor should you. Natural organic links would often be the domain name of the site only or perhaps a brand name, or even the classic click here. Try to make your links look natural in this way with a sprinkling of keyword rich anchor text. It is recommended when building your back links to restrict the use of your keywords in link text to less than 30% of the total links to your site, with the remainder being made up of your website name, website URL, your brand name, and generic terms (e.g. 'click here') in equal proportions.

Seek to obtain a good diversity in the types of website that link to yours including websites in the same or similar niche, social media sites, topic related discussion forums, relevant directories, and wikis. Links from educational sites with a '.edu' domain seem to be given a little extra weight by some search engines. Links from authority sites in a related niche are also of greater value for SEO.

While marketing your website online you may be tempted by ads promising you 1000's of back links to your website; these are the quickest way to get your site banned due to recent Google updates (2013 & 2014) as they are gained using spammy techniques and usually of low quality. Aim for quality over quantity when it comes to link building for your online business.

PageRank

Deciding upon what makes a *Quality Backlink* was at one time a simple matter of obtaining links from pages with a high PageRank. Things have however changed a great deal, with many other factors effecting how Google evaluates a link, including factors such as relevance, reputation and the quality of the linking website.

Whilst PageRank may have diminished in its own right with regard to overall ranking, it can still aid in your search for quality links as an *indicator* of the potential weight a link may offer if the previously mentioned attribute like relevance are also met.

What is PageRank?

In a nutshell incoming links pointing to a web page are considered editorial *votes* for the page. In addition, some links are considered more valuable than others. PageRank is Google's system for counting the votes (links) for a web page and uses them, combined with other factors, to determine how important or relevant a page may be.

Google's technology page states; "The heart of our software is PageRank™, a system for ranking web pages developed by our founders Larry Page and Sergey Brin at Stanford University. And while we have dozens of engineers working to improve every aspect of Google on a daily basis, PageRank continues to play a central role in many of our web search tools."

Understanding PageRank

PageRank relies on the democratic nature of the internet by using its huge link structure to indicate an individual page's value. In essence, a link from web page A to web page B is considered as a vote, by page A, for page B.

In reality, Google looks at many more factors than simply the sheer volume of votes, or links to a page; for example, it also analyzes the page containing the source of the link. Votes cast by web pages that are themselves considered important, provide more weight, helping to make other pages important.

Important, high-quality, and relevant pages usually receive a higher PageRank, which Google uses each time it conducts a search based on a users search query. Obviously Important pages mean nothing to you or a searcher if they don't match the context of your query. Therefore, Google combines the PageRank score with other algorithms and text-matching techniques to find web pages (or other content) that are both *important* and *relevant* to your search.

These days this text analysis goes far beyond the number of times a word or phrase appears on a particular page (Keyword Density), and combines dozens of additional ranking factors related to the page's content (and the content of those pages linking to it) to help determine if it is a good match for your search query and its position within search results. These factors include such subtleties as keywords on the linking page, the topic or nature of pages linking to the linking page, alternative word choices (on the target and linking page), and link location (links located towards the top of the content area are considered most relevant).

Google Toolbar PageRank

A common source of confusion among webmasters new to SEO is the difference between PageRank (PR) and the Google Toolbar PageRank *Score*. *PageRank* is a numeric value calculated using an equation based on incoming links, outbound links on a page, and a few other qualifiers, whereas *Google Toolbar PageRank* is an integer value that is a representation of a pages position in a scoring system ranked from 1 to 10. The difference is one represents the actual PageRank value (worth) of a page, and the latter scores a page compared to others on the internet. The Google Toolbar (and other websites and utilities) will generally provide a page Toolbar Rank rather than the actual PR of a page.

PageRank (PR) are the actual values (based on links) that Google uses as part of its internal ranking algorithm. These scores are constantly being updated as Google crawls the web. In contrast, the Toolbar PageRank is simply a snapshot of internal PageRank, ranked against other sites, and usually updated every few months. This update frequency is decreasing of late, with only two updates performed in 2013, the first in February and again just in time for Christmas.

When you first develop and launch your website you may well see a non-existent or very low Toolbar PageRank score for your website or web pages. Don't lose hope as this does not mean that your website is not collecting Internal PageRank credits; these will be reflected the next time a PR snapshot is performed and the Toolbar PageRank values are updated by Google. It's likely that after a few weeks you will have gained some PageRank, and may see an increase in traffic as a result, even though Google Toolbar PageRank will still display your old score. The frequency of updates to these numbers is decreasing and it is anticipated it will be phased out altogether in the near future.

Using PageRank

There is still a valid place within SEO for PageRank to be used to help evaluate the value of an incoming link, the key word here is *help*, rather than rely upon.

When taking into account the relevancy of a page, it should also be considered that a pages PR flows through the links on the page equally, that is to say that the total PR for a page is then divided among the outgoing links contained on the page, therefore a page containing many outgoing links will dilute the PR of the page, and pages with less outgoing links will pass more *Link Juice*. For this reason seeking links from pages based on PR alone is not sufficient, we should seek links from high PR ranking pages within our topic or niche that are not too heavily diluted by outgoing links.

In addition to outgoing links, you should also evaluate a websites quality as you would your own. Does the site only link out to relevant sites? Is the site free of spelling and other mistakes? Are there obvious errors with scripts or markup? Use your knowledge of evaluating the quality of your own web pages when deciding if another page makes the grade

There are a number of tools available allowing you to view the Toolbar PageRank of a web page, the first and most obvious is Google's own Toolbar, available for free from the search giant. There is also several plug-in utilities available for a number of browsers, including Firefox and Chrome, available from the appropriate plug-in or app store for your browser.

You could also use one of any number of websites that allow you to retrieve the Toolbar PageRank of any given web page or website URL, or even multiple pages, useful for checking out the competition!

PageRank Summary

PageRank calculates how important a page is, relatively speaking, compared to other pages on the web, based on links equating to votes for a page.

PageRank is just one of numerous factors used to determine the ranking and relevance of a web page or website in search engine result pages.

A high PageRank does *not* guarantee a high ranking in search results for any particular search term or keywords. If this were the case, sites with a Toolbar PageRank of 9 or 10 would dominate the result pages for any search you performed.

The anchor (clickable) text of a link is often far more important than if it is located on a high PR page. It is however extremely important not to have all of your links as keywords as this looks unnatural. Link around a third using your keywords, another third using a combination of website name and website address (e.g.thesite.com), with the final third made up of generic terms such as "Click Here" etc.

Another great way to find out which are the most relevant (and so best) pages to obtain links from is to think in terms of *search rank*. Perform a search for the words and phrases that you'd like your page to rank for and review the pages that appear highest in the search results. These results are what Google considers the most important and relevant pages, and those that you should seek to obtain links from. Why? Well, because Google is telling you that for the keyword or phrase that you searched for, these are what are considered the most relevant results. Links to your site from these will be the most productive, more so if you can obtain a link from a ".*org*", ".*gov*" or ".*edu*" domain as these carry additional weight and site authority status, as do older more established sites.

Submitting Your Website

The internet is full of search engines and web directories ready to add your link and send you free traffic. URL submission is the process of submitting your website URL for possible inclusion. This section provides some useful information for effective website submission,

How to Submit a Website URL

Before seeking out obscure web directories and search engines for site submission it is important to note that both Google and Bing offer website submission directly from your Webmasters Tools area. You should sign-up for, and take advantage of these search engine services before moving onto other URL submission tasks.

It is a good idea to make the distinction between web directories and search engines. Directory listings are usually provided by the submitter of the link, whereas search engines obtain data about your website by using software to crawl the pages of your site, often using your Title and Description SEO meta tags to add your link.

When submitting to web directories you should pay particular attention to relevance, ensuring you visit each directory manually to select the correct category for your website listing.

Use accurate and meaningful titles and descriptions that include your targeted keywords, where possible, during your website promotion activities. Don't forget to include a call-to-action in your description to increase click through rates.

URL Submission Mistakes

Avoid making some common site submission mistakes that can cost your site in terms of SEO and search rankings by following the guidelines below:

a) Do NOT use automated submission software, services or tools for your website submission, this is often seen as spam. Instead visit each website in turn and manually submit your pages directly.

b) Add your link to each directory using unique titles and descriptions each time that make sense, but also contain varying combinations of your main keywords.

c) Only submit your website to web directories that are relevant to your site, topic, or niche in some way. An incoming link from a pet care site to a car parts dealer is unlikely to offer much value.

d) Duplicate titles and descriptions may look like spam to some search engines. Use different combinations of your keywords and vary the text for your descriptions.

e) Do not enter page titles and descriptions in all uppercase, or use strange and unusual characters.

f) Keep page titles less than 60 characters in length.

g) Keep your page descriptions less than 140 characters.

h) Use only keyword tags related to your website. Unrelated tags are the very definition of spam!

i) Check your email account for confirmation links sent to you by the search engine or directory. It is therefore important to use a real email address. This can result in a lot of unwanted incoming emails so it is advised that you create an email address specifically for this task using one of a number of free email services available on the net.

j) Avoid submitting your website to web directories more than once. Be patient. Some directories can take months to review and allow your listing, but could send you to the back of the queue if you keep submitting.

k) Check the individual website submission policy before submitting deep page links, that is, links to pages within your site that are not your home page.

l) Check your submitted URL is typed correctly and presented in the format requested by the directory. In most cases this will be the fully qualified URL of your homepage; e.g. *http://www.yoursite.com*

URL Submission Sites

There are a number of important website submission sites that can help you add your link to web directories and search engines. Follow the submission guidelines shown above, with particular attention to unique titles and descriptions.

a) Submit URL to *Google* via your Webmasters Tools page (Do This FIRST)

b) Add your link to *Bing* Webmasters Tools (Do This NEXT)

c) Submit your site to *EntireWeb* (Multiple search engines)

d) Submit your URL to *Dmoz.org* (Open Directory Project)

Having submitted your site to the above sources it is time to go in search of directories that are somehow related to your niche or business. Links from related websites hold some value but links from unrelated websites can seem spammy. Use your favorite search engine to find relevant directories and submit your site, again using unique titles and descriptions for each submission.

Real World Promotion

It is important to continue to promote your website, or online business, both in the real physical world in addition to online in cyberspace.

Including your website URL on business cards and other business stationary is a good way to get the word out and depending upon the nature of your business, some well placed advertising in local newspapers or other publications could yield positive results.

As with any real world business, word of mouth is still a most excellent form of advertising, so don't forget to mention your website to your customers and encourage them to tell their friends or colleagues about you and the products or services that you offer.

SECTION 6 - ADVANCED SEO

Advanced Website Optimization

So you have completed your on-page SEO tasks, and your ongoing off page efforts are paying off, what more can be done with regards to website optimization to increase your search engine ranking and visibility?

While many webmasters may spend a great deal of time dealing with these regular internet marketing tasks, some may overlook some critical web SEO issues that could very well be effecting your search engine rankings, or perhaps making it difficult for search engine robots to crawl and index the individual pages contained on your site correctly.

This section aims to give an overview for some of these more obscure yet important website optimization issues and relates to your entire website as a whole, as opposed to *On-Page* SEO which is usually specific to a particular web page.

You should make testing your website(s) and blogs for these problems a part of your search engine optimization plan to ensure you really are achieving the best results with regard to your rankings.

Web Page Load Speeds

Currently a relatively minor search ranking factor (but a factor nonetheless), the speed that your web page(s) load for your visitors plays a huge part in your user experience and so page load speeds should be kept to a minimum.

Independent research has shown that many users will click away from a website delivering pages that take longer than 3 seconds to load, and so this figure would make a good maximum to work with. Both on-page and off-page factors may be effecting your page load times, or a combination of several.

Some potential causes of slow page load speeds may be;

a) Shared or unreliable website hosting service, or an overloaded web server.

b) Inferior server connection, server hardware or bad network management.

c) Large web page file size, or pages containing too many server-side included files (Scripts, CSS etc).

d) Large image file sizes, large number of images, or other large web page content that must be downloaded when the page is first displayed.

e) Pages with dead links to resources, images, scripts, or other support files.

f) Poorly written or unreliable server side scripts or web applications.

g) Shared or overloaded Database (DBMS) servers.

h) Overloaded or slow DNS servers.

i) Slow loading advertisements, social share buttons or other third party web page content.

Dealing in depth with these various website performance and setup issues is beyond the scope of this book, however for best SEO performance we suggest;

a) Use a reputable web hosting company for your website, ideally a dedicated server or VPS (Virtual Private Server) with a dedicated IP address for each website.

b) Use server side caching, where available, to speed up (cache) access times for frequently used pages.

c) Compress image file sizes using appropriate image compression/editing software.

d) Optimize CSS and JavaScript libraries into single files.

e) Split extra large web pages into separate topical pages.

f) Keep the total number of hyperlinks located on any one page below 100 and always strive for more standard text over anchor text on a page.

Authority Site Status

While you may have heard of *Google Page Rank*, largely based upon the number of external links pointing to a website, another very effective website optimization technique is to establish your website as an *authority site* within your niche.

There are no hard and fast rules to achieving authority site status as Google keeps these ranking signals under lock and key, but some worthwhile suggestions for achieving authority status include;

a) Obtaining a unique IP address for each of your websites.

b) Ensure your IP address is not hosting sites that search engines may frown upon (bad neighborhoods).

c) Link out only to valuable content and articles related to your topic or niche.

d) Provide an inviting user experience, simple navigation and good page load times.

e) Avoid spam (often referred to as 'black hat') website promotion techniques.

f) Use on-page SEO in accordance with Google *best practices* and those contained within this guide.

g) Try to become a hub of valuable information within your niche or chosen topic.

Content Markup Ratio

A *quality* signal that may have some impact on your website rankings is the ratio of markup on your page compared to actual text content. A page containing a lot of embedded styles and formatting (using the <style> tag to embed CSS for example), and excessive use of embedded JavaScript may cause an excessive loading time for a page that offers little quality content.

When stacked up against another website whose page offers similar content, without the page load time issue, the latter is likely to prevail and appear above your page in search results.

Reduce your page load times by combining all of your JavaScript libraries (where used) into a single .js file rather than calling numerous files when the page loads.

Also try to replace all internal embedded formatting with CSS (cascading style sheets), and again place them into a single .CSS file. The overall goal here is to reduce the total amount of formatting contained within the text of your page, while at the same time reduce the number of individual resources (files) that are loaded when the page first displayed. Most resources loaded within the <head> section of your page would qualify as this section is processed at the time the page is shown.

Website IP Address

The IP address of your website can impact your rankings to a varying degree. The worst type of penalty could be applied to a website that shares an IP address with another site that has been previously identified as hosting viruses or other types of malicious software. A lesser penalty could be applied to a site that shares an IP address with many other websites.

In terms of SEO and avoiding these potential penalties it makes sense to obtain a unique IP address for each of your sites. Most web hosting providers will offer these as an additional service on shared hosting, VPS and dedicated server packages.

To ensure your website always performs well it is recommended that you opt for the dedicated resources offered by virtual and dedicated server packages, over those of shared hosting services that may suffer from serious performance problems at busy times.

Secure Websites

In the later part of 2014, Google announced that it would be giving a slight ranking boost to secure websites, that is to say, websites secured (encrypted) with a SSL Certificate.

When a site utilizes a SSL Certificate (*Secure Socket Layer*) the data between the website and the user (and vice-versa) is encrypted for privacy. These encrypted pages are sent using the HTTPS protocol rather than the standard, non-encrypted HTTP protocol. The current protocol in use is shown at the start of a URL, as displayed in your browser address bar, e.g. https:// and http:// respectively. Most web browsers also indicate the presence of a secure connection with an additional status, padlock symbol, or by turning parts of the address bar green or amber.

A standard non secure connection
http://www.example.com

An encrypted secure connection
https://www.example.com

SSL Certificates should be used whenever sensitive or private information is transmitted over the internet and is an absolute must for e-commerce or other websites that conduct financial transactions online.

Even if you consider your website as content only, with no sensitive data involved, securing your site with SSL is still worth the investment as the current boost in rankings could soon become a penalty for sites that do not, at some point in the near future.

Setting up an SSL certificate is a two step process. You start by creating a Certificate Signing Request (CSR), created from your web server, and sent to the Certificate Authority you have purchased your certificate from. Your web host can help you with this. The second step is to install the certificate that you will be sent by email, onto your server. Once installed, all pages requested using the https:// prefix will be sent over a secure connection.

The use of SLL on our website does raise some issues related to duplicate content and our SEO efforts. When a page can be accessed via both a secure and non secure connection, these two separate pages may well be seen as duplicate pages, resulting in a negative impact on our search rankings.

To avoid these duplicate content issues on your website;

- Secure your entire website, not just sensitive sections. There seems little sense in not using a certificate if you have one to provide a secure browsing experience to your users, and failure to do so will cause complication and confusion regarding redirects;
- Change all links on your website from http:// to https:// if you have specified the protocol in your links. Also change the URLs for all of your images and other resources to reflect the new secure address.
- Redirect requests to the non secure http:// versions of the pages and resources to the new secure location using *301 Moved Permanently* redirect on your server.
- Ensure all of your secure pages *canonical tags* are updated to reflect the new https:// secure protocol.

Legal Matters

There are a number of *laws and regulations* governing the conduct of business on the Internet, privacy laws and other regulation that should be complied with during the operation of your day to day business.

Whilst business law is beyond the scope of this book, some aspects do hold some direct significance with regards to our SEO efforts and so we cover those here.

Legal Compliance

It is important for your business, and website, to comply with international and local laws, not just from a legal stand point but as an SEO quality issue also. Search engines may expect to find certain compliance issues to be dealt with on your website, and penalize your site if not compliant. One example where this could be an issue would be with a site based in the UK that stores private data in cookies. A law in the UK requires websites that use such cookies to obtain permission from the user, failure to do so could be seen as a site quality issue by search engines.

Copyright has become a big issue on the Internet in recent years and the use of copyrighted material on your website is another possible indicator of bad quality. A page full of unique quality images is likely to rank far better than a page containing copied material picked up on the internet. Furthermore, copyright complaints about your site sent directly to Google can cause you to hit a severe penalty until the offending material is removed from your site.

Terms & Privacy Policy

Another potential quality issue that is sometimes overlooked by webmasters is to provide a clear and easy to understand privacy policy. Whilst this is not a legal requirement, it is an expectation of any legitimate business operating a website to supply such details in an open manner.

You should also have a page dedicated to your terms and conditions of use for your website, alongside any other terms or conditions related to the purchase or use of your products, service or business.

Terms & Privacy Templates

We have created several templates that can be used to create your privacy and terms of use pages that you may edit to suit your particular needs. However, nothing beats good business legal advice, and so obtaining the services of a lawyer with regards to the content of such pages is encouraged. You can find a link to these free templates in the *Useful Resources* appendix towards the end of this book.

Internet Marketing Mistakes

While promoting your website or business there may be a number of mistakes that can be made with your online marketing that can directly affect the success of your business or internet enterprise.

Some mistakes can be caused by technical errors, others may be human error, or perhaps in some cases, as a result of bad promotion or SEO advice. In this section we explore some of the more common mistakes made by webmasters that could have a negative impact on your search engine rankings.

Mistake One: Low Quality Website Design

Your website is your business home on the internet. It is where you meet and interact with new potential customers. It is the one place where you must make your website visitors feel 'at home', quite literally. This should be the number one aim or goal of your website marketing online strategy.

Of course, you are a business that sells something, but merely selling your products or services without delivering a memorable customer experience for your visitors is a recipe for disaster. You need to ensure that every visitor to your website / online store remembers your brand, and your website, long after they leave your site.

Online business owners sometimes make the mistake of forgetting the importance of designing a website that reflects trust and professionalism. In a bid to spend less time, money or both, they end up with a website that makes little sense to the customer. Therefore, resist the temptation to save a few days or dollars, go for a quality website design that promises to deliver this message, while remaining straightforward and easy for your visitors to use.

Mistake Two: Lack of effective SEO

Some business owners may also believe that once they develop and launch a website, they are now free of worries and visitors will flow to their website or online store without putting in any extra effort. They may forget that stiff competition and the search results rankings play a major factor in online success and require constant attention and review.

Without making people aware of your existence in the market you cannot attract them as new customers. This is where SEO Search Engine Optimization plays a critical role. While some may claim that Internet marketing is not something you can do by yourself, we believe even the smallest online business can perform many of the required tasks as opposed to a professional SEO to take on the job of promoting your website and attracting a steady flow of new visitors.

If you do decide to rely on an SEO company or agency check that it has a reputation for working on business websites, delivering results within an acceptable time-frame and using techniques that do not breach the search engine webmaster guidelines.

Mistake Three: Duplicate Content Problems

Another online marketing mistake often overlooked by webmasters is the issue of duplicate content. Major search engines will list fresh unique content above stale, copied or duplicate content. Whilst this suggests that you should avoid stealing parts of other people's websites (scraping), it also extends to copying large blocks of your website to every page. Your navigation bars, header and footer etc are ok but avoid duplicating text in the actual content area of the web page.

Secondly, we have the problem of multiple names for the same piece of content. Is your website home page accessible using multiple URLs, e.g. *domain.com*, *www.domain.com* and *domain.com/index.html* variants? If so it is vital that these be setup the right way to avoid search engines seeing this as two (or more) duplicate websites, affecting the search engine rankings of all the pages involved.

The correct way to perform this is with the use of a '*301 Moved Permanently*' server *redirect,* whereby one location redirects the users browser to a single URL. For example; redirect all home page requests to www.domain.com no matter what variant is used. You should also redirect calls to your home page by its file name, for example; redirect all requests for the page *www.domain.com/index.html* to *www.domain.com* - Check your web hosting provider for details on setting up 301 Redirects.

If you have dynamic web pages that can be accessed via multiple URLs you should use the *rel="canonical"* tag to specify a single URL for the page or resource. This tag is placed into the <head> section of your page and takes the following form;

<link rel="canonical" href="http://www.domain.com/dynamicpage.asp?page=1">

Mistake Four: No Blog or Social Media Presence

Social signals from social networking sites and blogs are playing an increasing role with major search engine rankings. In addition to creating a blog with great content to encourage social shares, you should consider setting up pages with the top social networks and linking to your pages from your website and blog.

Don't forget to include a link to your website on your social pages. We have seen an increase in rankings by adopting this cross linking marketing strategy.

Mistake Five: Ineffective Call to Action / Closing Sales

The desired outcome of all marketing online is conversion, turning potential customers into actual customers. Business owners forget that without a good, clear and effective Call-to-action (CTA), all internet marketing efforts go in vain.

An effective CTA is just as important as having a good product or service. Unless your call to action initiates the desired action, your website is not going to generate leads or sell any products. Every CTA must resonate with the offerings contained on the page. Avoid using random CTA buttons or text such as 'Submit', 'Click Here', etc., instead, design related and clear calls to action that are effective and prompt website visitors to take the specific action you want.

Mistake Six: Lack of Visitor Tracking / Analysis

Businesses may also suffer from a failure to implement and utilize *Analytic* and *Visitor Tracking*. Without using analytic software, it is impossible to track your web site visitors, identify which web pages are generating the most (and least) traffic, pages that produce sales and conversions plus other important visitor patterns.

This valuable insight into your website visitor behavior can be used it to identify the best pages and best performing sections of your website that generate the least or most traffic, sales, conversions, even track offer pages.

After reviewing this data you can make the necessary changes to badly performing web pages, or sections of your website, in order to attract and retain more leads and customers.

Google Analytics is a very popular free website analytic and tracking service that can be implemented into your website by simply adding some HTML code to each of the web pages that you wish to track.

Mistake Seven: Dishonest Practices

While conducting business online you might be tempted to adopt get-rich quick attitude. You may adapt various underhand techniques, including exaggerating facts and features so that the potential new customers are lured to buy your product or services.

You could publish fake testimonials and reviews, highlight features that don't exist, or promise something and deliver something else to increase your sales. This might work in the short term, when people discover that you are not being honest; you will have a lot of problems on your hands.

Do not opt for short-term gimmicks and tricks. Adapt a proper, long term internet marketing strategy. Promise your customers only what you can deliver. Online marketing is not about earning profits in the short term, it is about earning trust and building a reputation, which will ultimately lead to increase in sales in the long term.

Mistake Eight: Lack of Consistent Online Marketing

Internet marketing is a long term form of online advertising. It is a slow and steady, ongoing process, however business owners may sometimes lose their focus and interest in the tasks related to their internet marketing efforts. They get bored, busy, or become less faithful about internet marketing.

Webmasters and business owners must avoid this type of mistake. You must be consistent with your online marketing efforts in order to achieve effective and sustained results. The expectation that your product sales will sky-rocket within the first few weeks of your online marketing campaign is not a realistic one. It takes some time for people to become aware of your brand, product and service, especially when other brands are fighting for their attention on the internet.

Keep your focus on your internet marketing plan, avoid the online marketing mistakes shown above and your efforts and investment will pay-off, but only if you continue to promote your website and brand consistently.

SECTION 7 - SEO IN THE FUTURE

The world of *search engine optimization* is a forever changing landscape. With major indexes such as Google releasing regular updates to its algorithm, pretty much on a daily basis, it helps to understand the general direction that search engines are headed and use this information to predict further potential changes that could effect your website.

Search Context

In the future Search engines will without a doubt improve upon the current contextual nature of a search, or indeed multiple searches, in an aim to deliver more relevant results to the end user.

More and more searches are presented in the form of a question as opposed to just keywords when users perform a search, and search engines seek to provide an actual answer where possible, instead of a blind result based solely upon website content and exact match keyword phrases. With the aid of *semantics*, search engines will look increasingly to ascertain the actual intent of a search and produce relevant results.

Recent updates have indeed looked to improve this type of search and the results can be seen for example by performing a query such as 'Show me pictures of London' and this is exactly what you will get. If you then perform the query 'what is London?' you would usually be presented with a wikipedia definition of London followed by other relevant results.

It is anticipated that a large number of search engine updates in the near future will be related to refining this type of semantic search.

If your page answers a question, including that question text within the text of your page would certainly be a good idea, but above all look at the quality of the information you provide. Is it up to date, accurate, complete and concise?

Search Synonyms

Set to play an increasing role in the future of SEO are search *synonyms*. Modern search engines understand the meaning of words and can produce results for pages that do not heavily target the particular word or phrase that was originally queried by the user.

For example, suppose we enter the search term 'auto insurance' we will get back a list of results that would be similar to the query 'car insurance' and not just pages that target the word auto.

Including alternative keywords and phrases that have the same meaning within your text will not only help you gain potential traffic via these additional keywords but also help you avoid the overuse of your main keywords, and the potential penalty that could follow in extreme cases. It also makes your text more readable to a human user, increasing the overall quality of the page.

Mobile Search

It is now usual practice for many people to use multiple devices, sometimes simultaneously, to access the internet. I myself have been known to edit an article on my desktop PC, from research displayed on a tablet, while staying in touch with friends on Facebook and twitter via my smart phone. Two of the three activities are using mobile devices in this instance and this trend is set to continue to grow.

It is now commonplace for content designed for mobiles to be given priority in search results where the search is originating from a mobile device and so it will become increasingly important to ensure that your content is mobile friendly.

Responsive content (as Google refers to it) is content that is repackaged to offer the best user experience based upon the device requesting it. This can be achieved in one of two ways; the use of cascading style sheets (CSS) with separate styles defined for different devices, or by the creation of a specific site designed for mobiles, for example; *'m.facebook.com'* is the mobile friendly version of Facebook whereas *'www.facebook.com'* is the full desktop site.

Google has now started to notify mobile searchers if a destination site in search results contains content that cannot be displayed on a mobile device, like Flash and Java applets, resulting in fewer clicks for such sites. It is possible these sites could be penalized, or removed from mobile search results completely, at some point in the future.

Check out some of the tools available on the web that allow you to view your website in various formats and devices, and ensure your website is easy to use and navigate on all platforms.

Social Search

In 2010 both Google and Bing confirmed that Facebook and Twitter activity effects search results. Google in particular also favors sites with +1's and *authorship* that links Google+ users to content they have created. Whilst the bonus feature of authorship, namely to have your Google+ profile picture shown next to your listing, has now been removed, this does not mean the value of authorship has diminished in any way with regard to the SEO benefits.

The type of social activity that affects search results would include the number of likes that your page(s) receive, shares of your website links and social content, plus user engagement such as user comments on your posts.

Due to the ever increasing nature of social signals in SEO, and the expansion of social networks, along with the role they play in peoples lives, your social media efforts should be an ongoing task looking to leverage your social presence by engaging and interacting with your audience on a regular basis rather than using your social platform simply as another billboard or sales platform.

SECTION 8 - TOP TEN SEO TIPS

SEO (Search Engine Optimization) has become a crucial part of Internet Marketing to ensure that your website is easily found by potential new customers, and so we have put together a Top 10 SEO Tips checklist to help you get the best search results for your website or online business.

Operating an online business, website, or e-commerce store requires that your site to be easily found in the major search engines. Just as retail stores try to get the best operating location, websites need to rank well in search engine results to be successful.

The following Top 10 SEO tips are simple but highly effective techniques that can be used to improve your website search engine rankings to boost traffic, and ultimately, sales.

TIP ONE: Quality Incoming Links

By far the top SEO tip would be to encourage high authority, industry and niche related websites to link to the pages on your website. This is an important factor in optimizing your site in search engine results. Quality inbound links from other websites and blogs help search engines find your website and understand what your web pages are about. In addition to the traffic these links may bring, many search engines will also treat these links as editorial votes for your site, and the more votes you have from quality related sites, the better your site will perform in search result pages.

TIP TWO: Keyword Research

Do some extensive keywords research for your website and investigate; who is your target market? What keywords or phrases do they most often use to search for your products or services on the Internet? Concentrate on keywords related to your niche market or demographics. Construct a list of keywords and phrases to target your SEO and work them into your websites Meta Tags and web page content as described earlier in this book.

TIP THREE: Include Quality Text Information

Search engines look for informative text on your website to understand the topic of your web pages and return useful, quality information in search result pages. Search engines can't read image files, Videos and animations etc, so they need normal informative text. Give search engines plenty of relevant text to read, including your keywords and phrases to enhance your SEO. An additional benefit of providing quality, useful and helpful information on your website is that other site owners are more likely to link to your content, and you will rewarded for these additional inbound links.

TIP FOUR: Incorporate Keywords

Use your keywords for SEO in the content of your web pages. Incorporate your keywords into the text of your pages, in moderation, by adding relevant text to; heading tags, internal and external links, image titles and descriptions, and the description and keyword meta tags of your web pages.

TIP FIVE: Create Unique Content

Ensure each of your web pages has a unique *title* and contains unique content. Each of your pages should have its own unique content, plus the keywords and title you choose for each page should reflect the content of the page. For best SEO each page should have a different focus or emphasis. It is important to have a different title for each web page as search engines rank web pages, not websites. Also, search engines will punish websites that copy other content from other locations, therefore always produce your own unique and distinct content for your site.

TIP SIX: Fresh Updated Content

Update the text content of your website and blog on a regular basis. Search engines try to deliver the best quality, up-to-date and relevant information to people searching the Internet, favoring websites that are updated regularly with fresh, quality content and rewarding this with higher search rankings.

TIP SEVEN: Interactive Content

Add interactive content and features to your website. Give your site visitors the opportunity to add comments, chat with each other, submit product reviews, and vote in polls, or share links and images via social networking sites. These interactive features encourage visitors to return and tell others about your website. These social signals also attract the attention of search engines. Interactive content such as chat software, discussion forums and blogs also encourage site visitors to generate more fresh content for your site.

TIP EIGHT: Check Out The Competition

Look at your competitors' website content, and the web pages that appear first in the search result for your chosen keyword(s). Watch the search results to see which pages perform well for your target keywords consistently. How does your competitor use these keywords and phrases on their ranking pages or as part of an SEO strategy? How are the links and text structured? How much information do they offer and in what formats? Does your site use a similar structure?

TIP NINE: Do Not Spam

The days of using automated software to post thousands of blog comments containing your website link in order to increase rankings are over. With Google's *Penguin* and *Panda* updates the days of SEO ranking for low quality links have come to an end, along with another form of web spam, namely keyword stuffing. Keyword stuffing is where an unusual amount of related, or in some case, not related keywords, are placed onto a page simply in an attempt to rank for those phrases.

Today, these types of Black Hat website promotion techniques will at best do you no good, and at worst get your website banned from the search engine altogether!

To avoid the wrath of the search engines, only use keywords in moderation, and in context, and only seek links from quality sources and authority site. We have ranked websites recently with less than 20 links; it's all about quality not quantity of inbound links.

TIP TEN: Track Your Visitors

Use analytic and website statistics to learn what sites and pages are driving traffic to your website, and which pages on your website are the most popular and best performing. Once armed with this vital marketing information you can seek to improve problem areas of your site and concentrate your efforts on website promotion that works well, dropping less effective promotional channels.

SECTION 9 - TROUBLESHOOTING

Black Hat Hurts!

Black Hat is an industry term used to describe spam techniques that are designed to game the search engines. Purchasing links to your website is one such practice that search engines frown upon.

The days of using automated software, to post thousands of blog and forum comments containing your keyword heavy website link, in order to game search engines and increase rankings are over. With the coming of Google's *Penguin* and *Panda* updates the days of ranking from low quality links have come to an end, along with another form of web spam, namely keyword stuffing.

Keyword stuffing is the practice of using an unusual amount of related, or in some case, not related keywords, that are placed onto a page simply in an attempt to rank for those phrases.

Today, these types of *Black Hat* website promotion techniques will at best do you no good, perhaps get you penalized, and at worst get your website banned from the search engine altogether!

To avoid the wrath of the search engines, use keywords in moderation only, keeping them in context, and only seek links from quality sources and authority site. We have ranked websites recently with less than 20 links; it's all about quality not quantity of inbound links.

Never use unrelated keywords in an attempt to drive more traffic to your website. Search engines will notice this, and take action against you, leaving you not ranking well for either the out of place, or your targeted keywords. Only ever target keywords directly related to the topic or niche of the page.

If you have followed the advice set forth in this book and are still having problems ranking your website for your targeted keywords after a number of weeks have elapsed, it could be due to a number of common mistakes made by webmasters, or in some cases, agents previously employed by a website to help with search rankings, who may have used frowned upon techniques that are now penalized, or no longer of help.

In addition to the common mistakes that follow, it may be tempting to take up offers of 'first page rankings on Google' offered by less than scrupulous SEO companies, usually via spam emails, using frowned upon techniques. Only Google could make such a guarantee, and even if successful in the short term, the effects will be short lived, and depending upon the techniques used, could result in a removal of your listing completely.

It is far better to establish a long term element of trust with search engines by avoiding the use of any such techniques, implementing the safe advice contained in this book, and providing high quality and useful content to your website visitors, rather than address the manpower and resources required to regain this trust (and your ranking) once it has been lost!

Common Mistakes

While promoting your website or business there may be a number of mistakes that can be made with your online marketing that can directly affect the success of your business or internet enterprise.

Some mistakes can be caused by technical errors, others may be human error, or perhaps in some cases, as a result of bad promotion or SEO advice. In this section we explore some of the more common mistakes made by webmasters that could have a negative impact on your search engine rankings.

1: Low Quality Website Design

Your website is your business home on the internet. It is where you meet and interact with new potential customers. It is the one place where you must make your website visitors feel 'at home', quite literally. This should be the number one aim or goal of your website marketing online strategy.

Of course, you are a business that sells something, but merely selling your products or services without delivering a memorable customer experience for your visitors is a recipe for disaster. You need to ensure that every visitor to your website / online store remembers your brand, and your website, long after they leave your site.

Online business owners sometimes make the mistake of forgetting the importance of designing a website that reflects trust and professionalism. In a bid to spend less time, money or both, they end up with a website that makes little sense to the customer. Therefore, resist the temptation to save a few days or dollars, go for a quality website design that promises to deliver this message, while remaining straightforward and easy for your visitors to use.

2: Lack of effective SEO

Some business owners may also believe that once they develop and launch a website, they are now free of worries and visitors will flow to their website or online store without putting in any extra effort. They may forget that stiff competition and the search results rankings play a major factor in online success and require constant attention and review.

Without making people aware of your existence in the market you cannot attract them as new customers. This is where SEO Search Engine Optimization plays a critical role. While some may claim that Internet marketing is not something you can do by yourself, we believe even the smallest online business can perform many of the required tasks as opposed to a professional SEO to take on the job of promoting your website and attracting a steady flow of new visitors.

If you do decide to rely on an SEO company or agency check that it has a reputation for working on business websites, delivering results within an acceptable time-frame and using techniques that do not breach the search engine webmaster guidelines.

3: Duplicate Content Problems

Another online marketing mistake often overlooked by webmasters is the issue of duplicate content. Major search engines will list fresh unique content above stale, copied or duplicate content. Whilst this suggests that you should avoid stealing parts of other people's websites (scraping), it also extends to copying large blocks of your website to every page. Your navigation bars, header and footer etc are ok but avoid duplicating text in the actual content area of the web page.

Secondly, we have the problem of multiple names for the same piece of content. Is your website home page accessible using multiple URLs, e.g. *domain.com*, *www.domain.com* and *domain.com/index.html* variants? If so it is vital that these be setup the right way to avoid search engines seeing this as two (or more) duplicate websites, affecting the search engine rankings of all the pages involved.

The correct way to perform this is with the use of a '*301 Moved Permanently*' server *redirect,* whereby one location redirects the users browser to a single URL. For example; redirect all home page requests to www.domain.com no matter what variant is used. You should also redirect calls to your home page by its file name, for example; redirect all requests for the page *www.domain.com/index.html* to *www.domain.com* - Check your web hosting provider for details on setting up 301 Redirects.

If you have dynamic web pages that can be accessed via multiple URLs you should use the *rel="canonical"* tag to specify a single URL for the page or resource. This tag is placed into the <head> section of your page and takes the following form;

<link rel="canonical" href="http://www.domain.com/dynamicpage.asp?page=1">

4: No Blog or Social Media Presence

Social signals from social networking sites and blogs are playing an increasing role with major search engine rankings. In addition to creating a blog with great content to encourage social shares, you should consider setting up pages with the top social networks and linking to your pages from your website and blog.

Don't forget to include a link to your website on your social pages. We have seen an increase in rankings by adopting this cross linking marketing strategy.

5: Ineffective Call to Action / Closing Sales

The desired outcome of all marketing online is conversion, turning potential customers into actual customers. Business owners forget that without a good, clear and effective Call-to-action (CTA), all internet marketing efforts go in vain.

An effective CTA is just as important as having a good product or service. Unless your call to action initiates the desired action, your website is not going to generate leads or sell any products. Every CTA must resonate with the offerings contained on the page. Avoid using random CTA buttons or text such as 'Submit', 'Click Here', etc., instead, design related and clear calls to action that are effective and prompt website visitors to take the specific action you want.

6: Lack of Visitor Tracking / Analysis

Businesses may also suffer from a failure to implement and utilize *Analytic* and *Visitor Tracking*. Without using analytic software, it is impossible to track your web site visitors, identify which web pages are generating the most (and least) traffic, pages that produce sales and conversions plus other important visitor patterns.

This valuable insight into your website visitor behavior can be used it to identify the best pages and best performing sections of your website that generate the least or most traffic, sales, conversions, even track offer pages.

After reviewing this data you can make the necessary changes to badly performing web pages, or sections of your website, in order to attract and retain more leads and customers.

Google Analytics is a very popular free website analytic and tracking service that can be implemented into your website by simply adding some HTML code to each of the web pages that you wish to track.

7: Dishonest Practices

While conducting business online you might be tempted to adopt get-rich quick attitude. You may adapt various underhand techniques, including exaggerating facts and features so that the potential new customers are lured to buy your product or services.

You could publish fake testimonials and reviews, highlight features that don't exist, or promise something and deliver something else to increase your sales. This might work in the short term, when people discover that you are not being honest; you will have a lot of problems on your hands.

Do not opt for short-term gimmicks and tricks. Adapt a proper, long term internet marketing strategy. Promise your customers only what you can deliver. Online marketing is not about earning profits in the short term, it is about earning trust and building a reputation, which will ultimately lead to increase in sales in the long term.

8: Lack of Consistent Online Marketing

Internet marketing is a long term form of online advertising. It is a slow and steady, ongoing process, however business owners may sometimes lose their focus and interest in the tasks related to their internet marketing efforts. They get bored, busy, or become less faithful about internet marketing.

Webmasters and business owners must avoid this type of mistake. You must be consistent with your online marketing efforts in order to achieve effective and sustained results. The expectation that your product sales will sky-rocket within the first few weeks of your online marketing campaign is not a realistic one. It takes some time for people to become aware of your brand, product and service, especially when other brands are fighting for their attention on the internet.

Keep your focus on your internet marketing plan, avoid the online marketing mistakes shown above and your efforts and investment will pay-off, but only if you continue to promote your website and brand consistently.

9: URL Submission

Avoid making some common site submission mistakes that can cost your site in terms of SEO and search rankings by following the guidelines below:

a) Do NOT use automated submission software, services or tools for your website submission, this is often seen as spam. Instead visit each website in turn and manually submit your pages directly.

b) Add your link to each directory using unique titles and descriptions each time that make sense, but also contain varying combinations of your main keywords.

c) Only submit your website to web directories that are relevant to your site, topic, or niche in some way. An incoming link from a pet care site to a car parts dealer is unlikely to offer much value.

d) Duplicate titles and descriptions may look like spam to some search engines. Use different combinations of your keywords and vary the text for your descriptions.

e) Do not enter page titles and descriptions in all uppercase, or use strange and unusual characters.

f) Keep page titles less than 60 characters in length.

g) Keep page descriptions less than 140 characters.

h) Use only keyword tags related to your website. Unrelated tags are the very definition of spam!

i) Check your email account for confirmation links sent to you by the search engine or directory. It is therefore important to use a real email address. This can result in a lot of unwanted incoming emails so it is advised that you create an email address specifically for this task using one of a number of free email services available on the net.

j) Avoid submitting your website to web directories more than once. Be patient. Some directories can take months to review and allow your listing, but could send you to the back of the queue if you keep submitting.

k) Check the individual website submission policy before submitting deep page links, that is, links to pages within your site that are not your home page.

l) Check your submitted URL is typed correctly and presented in the format requested by the directory. In most cases this will be the fully qualified URL of your homepage; e.g. *http://www.yoursite.com*

ALGORITHM PENALTIES

In this section we examine the specifics of the most important updates to Google's algorithm that could cost your website ranking positions, due to automatic penalties placed upon it.

If you have a website that has been around a while, you should double check that none of your previous SEO activities (or those conducted on your behalf) has not triggered a penalty, or indeed could in the future.

If you are developing a new site you should make yourself aware of these new rules and implement the recommended guidance into your development to avoid any such penalties in the future.

Panda Update

Google Panda is a *significant* change to Google's search ranking algorithm that was first released in February 2011. The change is focuses on lowering the rank of *low-quality* websites (or *thin sites*), and return the higher-quality sites nearer to the top of the search results.

Some providers reported a surge in the rankings for news related websites and social networking sites, and a drop in rankings for sites containing large amounts of advertising.

This update was reported to have affected the rankings of almost 12 percent of all search results, one of the widest reaching updates to date.

Soon after the Panda update rollout, Google's webmaster forum became filled with complaints of scrapers/copyright infringers getting better rankings than the sites containing the original content, and at one point, Google publicly asked for data points to help detect scrapers.

Panda has received several updates since the original rollout, and the effect went global in April 2011. To help affected website owners and publishers, Google provided an advisory on its blog, giving some clear direction for self-evaluation of a website's quality. They have provided a list of points on its blog answering the question "*What is a high-quality site*?", designed to help webmasters peek into Google's mindset.

Panda was a significant algorithm update that used artificial intelligence in a more sophisticated and scalable way. *Human* quality testers rated thousands of sites based on various aspects of quality, including site design, trustworthiness, website speed, and whether or not they would return to the website. Google's new machine-learning algorithm was then used to look for similarities between websites people found to be high quality and low quality.

Many new ranking signals have been introduced to the Google algorithm as a result, while older, less intelligent ranking factors such as PageRank have been downgraded in weight as a ranking signal.

Panda is updated from time to time and the algorithm is run on the Google network on a regular basis. In April 2012 the Google *Penguin* update was rolled-out, affecting a further 3.1% of all English search queries.

In September 2012, a Panda update was confirmed by Google via its official Twitter page, where it announced; *"Panda refresh is rolling out - expect some flux over the next few days. Fewer than 0.7% of queries noticeably affected".*

Another Panda update was released in January 2013, affecting about 1.2% of English queries.

Panda vs Previous Algorithms

Google Panda affects the ranking of an entire website, or even a specific section of a site, as opposed to targeting specific individual pages.

In March 2012, Google updated Panda and stated that they were deploying an *"over-optimization penalty,"* in order to level the playing field.

Panda Recovery

Google says that it only takes a few pages on a site containing poor quality or duplicative content to hold down your rankings (and traffic) on an otherwise good quality site, and recommends such low quality pages be removed from the site, blocked from being indexed by the search engine, or rewritten, and must be of a sufficiently high quality, as such content brings "additional value" to the web.

Website content that is broad or general, non-specific, and not substantially different from what is already available on the web should not be expected to rank well: Those sites are not bringing any additional value.

The key to recovery here seems obvious; fill our websites with fresh, unique and high quality content that has not been begged, borrowed or stolen from elsewhere. Bring something new by adding value in some way with unique insights, reviews, related facts and resources.

Prevent all pages that do not offer such high quality content from being indexed by search engines using meta tags in your pages, or a robots.txt file.

Penguin Update

Penguin is a Google algorithm update that was first announced in April 2012. Aimed at decreasing search engine rankings for websites that violate Google's *Webmaster Guidelines,* by using black-hat SEO techniques designed to artificially increase the ranking of a webpage, by manipulating the number of incoming links pointing to the page. These tactics are often described as link schemes or link networks.

By Google's own estimates, the Penguin update affects approximately 3% of search queries in English, about 3% of queries in languages like German, Chinese, and Arabic, and an even bigger percentage of sites within "highly spammed" niches.

In May 2012, Google rolled-out another Penguin update, Penguin 1.1. This update was predicted to affect less than one-tenth of a percent of all English searches. The principle goal for the update was to penalize websites found to be using manipulative techniques to achieve high rankings.

The purpose for Google was to catch excessive spammers, but it seems that some legitimate websites may have been caught with this latest algorithm change.

A few websites lost search rankings on Google for specific keywords during the *Panda* and *Penguin* rollouts. It appears anchor text was to blame in many of these cases, as the links pointing to these sites concentrated on only several specific keywords. While the content of the websites may have been satisfactory, as the update focused heavily on the quality of incoming links, the overall impact varied for different websites.

Google specifically mentions that doorway pages, those pages that are only built to attract search engine traffic, are against their webmaster guidelines. Regardless of this, many people still use this technique to target additional keywords, but should be mindful that Google has this technique clearly in its sights for action.

Penguin 3 was released in October 2012 and affected 0.3% of queries. Matt Cutts, leader of Google's web spam team, announced on May 10, 2013 that the next major Penguin update would sport the name Penguin 2.0.

Penguin vs Previous Algorithms

Before *Penguin*, Google released a series of algorithm updates called Panda (see previous section) with the first appearing in February 2011. Panda aimed at lowering the ranking of websites that provided poor user experience. The algorithm implements a system by which Google's human quality raters determine the quality of a website.

In January 2012, the *Page Layout Algorithm* update was released, targeting websites with little content, or too much advertising above the fold (the area of a web page that can be viewed without scrolling).

The strategic goals that Panda, Penguin, and the Page Layout updates all share is to bump up and display higher quality websites at the top of Google's search results. However, sites that were down-ranked as the result of these updates have different characteristics.

Two days after the initial Penguin update was rolled-out Google delivered a feedback form, designed for two type of users; those who want to report web spam that is still ranking highly after the algorithm change, and those who think that their site was unfairly penalized by the update. Google also has a reconsideration request form, available through Google Webmaster Tools for the 700,000 affected sites.

Penguin Recovery

Does your site use doorway pages to attract more traffic? It could be time to rethink think this strategy as you could be losing more traffic through a penguin penalty than you gain through the extra keywords. Replace these doorway pages with quality unique content that has some value, and target those pages to the extra keywords you need. Where adding fresh valuable content is not an option, these pages should be removed, returning a 404 response code to ensure search engines know this page no longer exists.

Do not bog down the top of your pages with lots of advertising as this leads to a poor user experience. Instead, place your most critical information (text containing your targeted keywords) as close to the top of the page as possible. Advertising should take up a secondary position on the page and not be excessive in number. Too many more than 2-3 ads on a page could start to cost you quality points.

When building incoming links to your site it is important to create a *natural* looking link profile. The overuse of your main keywords within the anchor text of incoming links will subject you to a penalty, and in some extreme cases, a manual action, or perhaps even the complete de-indexing of the site.

An ideal ratio for link anchor text is to target around a third of your links to use your keywords, another third should be your website or brand name, with the final third of your links using generic text such as click here, more etc.

If you have participated in link schemes, networks, or paid for links, you should start the task of removing these links, ideally at the source, but failing that, via the Link Disavow tool.

Concentrate on building high quality back links only from relevant, well respected, highly ranked, authority websites within your niche. The game is now about link quality and not so much about link quantity. Low quality links can actually harm your rankings, but it seems you do not need too many high quality backlinks in order to rank well.

Hummingbird Update

To celebrate its 15th birthday, Google held a press conference to announce the launch of a new *Hummingbird* algorithm update, claiming that Google search can now be a more humane way to interact with users and provide a more direct answer to a user natural language query.

Google suggests that its hummingbird algorithm has gradually abandoned the traditional model, allowing users a more natural ways to use search engines.. Google has said that this is the largest algorithm update in three years with the last update three years prior, the *caffeine plan*.

Google search engine can now make use of more complex search requests with a better understanding of human language, rather than a few scattered words. Google stated that such an algorithm improvement is necessary because the available data shows that many users enter a query in the search box to search the complete questions, to which Google wishes to return a valid result, e.g. answer the question.

Also as more and more Internet users access the web via smart-phones and tablet devices, they will often enter through a complete interrogative voice tool, in which the motive for this Google algorithm update lies.

There are two innovations designed to return the answer to the user, rather than to reflect a simple set of search results: The new engine has a better contrast filter - which can help users through mobile devices with Google to achieve a more natural conversation.

With the new filters, users can order his phone to "Tell me more about Impressionist artist information," Google can provide more background information such artist, genre, or other relevant or useful content.

In addition, the current design assumes a different intent role in the mobile space than within desktop space. Google promised to provide mobile search applications a "more unified design," and highlighted for the user to provide answers, rather than search results.

Google Now, with the emergence of the hummingbird algorithm, increasingly see themselves as an agent that can naturally interact with users, not just a portal leading to other websites. Google research and development department in the future may be more ambitious with its goals, perhaps providing medical diagnostics and personalized voting guide, or even "Why are we here?"

Hummingbird Recovery

This update does not really represent a penalty, but more an improvement to Google's search results, that could displace your site somewhat in the rankings. Certainly it would seem that we can improve our chances of ranking higher by developing two versions of our website, one for mobiles and optimized for the type of mobile search that hummingbird addresses, and our main website optimized for more traditional type searches.

MANUAL PENALTIES

Identify Manual Penalties

Previously, the primary focus of this chapter has been to provide the tools and information required to avoid any **Algorithmic Penalties** that could be placed on your website by search engines. Following the advice in this book should help you avoid any such penalties, and taking the corrective action outlined in previous sections should help you recover from these, once search engines have crawled and indexed your new website content and found the *quality links* that point at your site.

However, there is another form of penalty that could be place upon your site that will have a serious impact on your rankings, or perhaps remove you from the index altogether. This more critical type of sanction, a **Manual Action** by Google's web spam team, can spell the sudden death of a previously well ranking website.

If you have followed good practices, or have created a new web site based upon the advice presented so far in this book it is unlikely you will be affected by these issues, however there was a time when some of these bad practices were actively practiced by webmasters because they *did* produce results. Something that created a boost in rankings a year or two ago could be the very thing that caused your rankings to fall off the cliff into obscurity.

Readers who may have participated in such black hat techniques can use the information presented in this section to try and recover from a drop in rankings, but new webmasters should also review the information here in order to avoid falling into this very deep hole of obscurity.

Checking for Manual Actions

The first step to recovery is to identify; if a manual action has been taken against your site (as opposed to an algorithmic penalty), and the initial cause of this action.

The place to acquire this information is Google's Web Master Tools (WMT). You should already have an account, if you don't it is vital that you create one in order to monitor your traffic, and receive important notices about your website, including any manual actions that may have been taken against your site.

1. Visit http://www.google.com/webmasters/
2. Log-on with your username and password.
3. Select your website in the confirmed sites list.
4. Click *Search Traffic* in the menu on the left.
5. Select *Manual Actions* from the expanded list.
6. Review the supplied information.

Hopefully, if you have followed good practices, you will see the message "**No manual webspam actions found**". This indicates that there are no manual actions against your site.

If you are presented with any message(s) other than the one shown above, then you have a serious problem that requires immediate attention by following the steps in the remaining sections of this chapter.

Cleaning Up

Manual actions are very different from an Algorithmic penalty as a manual action is imposed directly by Google's web spam team, who constantly watch out for black hat techniques and will sanction webmasters who have employed any technique that falls outside of Google's webmaster guidelines.

Here we will examine some of the more common manual action notices that you may receive, the effect it may have on your website health (*symptom*), why you have been sanctioned (*cause*), and steps you can take towards a solution and recovery (*treatment*).

Common Manual Actions

"Unnatural links to your site"

Cause: Bad incoming links from irrelevant sites, other languages sites, spammy article directories, paid links, low quality directories, PR sites, and social bookmarking. Could also include; site wide links, link farms, reciprocal links, and 3 way linking etc.

Symptom: If you have received this notice from Google then the chances are high that your website traffic must have fallen from the top of a cliff, and in my experience these sites witness a drop in organic traffic, in some cases, of over 90%. This is one notice that no webmaster would like to see in his lifetime as it is one of the most difficult, and time consuming, to deal with and effectively recover from, leading to a prolonged period of massively reduced traffic.

Treatment: There is no quick fix remedy or solution for this type of manual action. You need to do a backlink audit by downloading all of the incoming back links from Google webmaster tools by selecting *'Links to Your Site'* in the *Search Traffic* section, and clicking on the *'more..'* link located underneath the area titled *'Who links the most'*. You will need to cleanup the bad quality links including; all irrelevant links, article links, paid links, low quality directories, PR sites, social bookmarking, site wide links and link farms.

You will need to contact the webmasters or website owners of these bad links and request that they remove these links. Follow up with an additional request in a couple of days if the link is not removed and send remainders.

Wait for around two weeks after your first link removal request date and then disavow all bad links using the Google disavow tool (see the next section *Recovery & Reconsideration*). After disavowing all of your bad links, send a detailed reconsideration request to Google. The entire process may take a number of weeks before you can expect Google to take any action.

Warning: Do not disavow *ALL* of your incoming links. If you do you will indeed have your penalty revoked, but your site will not get back the previous rankings and traffic it once enjoyed as not all of these links will be 'bad'. If you use a service provider for your SEO you should review and confirm the disavow file before submitting it.

"Unnatural links to your site-Impact sites"

Cause: This notice is given due to a pattern of unnatural backlinks, paid link networks, unnatural, artificial, deceptive, or manipulative links. This is a way of Google telling you that your participation in these types of link networks that pass page rank has been detected.

Symptom: Same as for "*Unnatural links to your site*"

Treatment: You may have purchased these links by yourself or perhaps hired an agency or freelancer to build links for you or do SEO. If you have paid for links you should consider removing them immediately.

Instruct your service provider (if you have one) to stop all link building activities and remove these problematic links.

After removing all paid links you will need to send a reconsideration request to Google explaining the situation, and the steps you have taken to remedy.

Warning: If any of these bad links generate real traffic to your website you should consider using a *"rel=nofollow"* parameter within the links anchor tag for those links. This parameter instructs Google to ignore this link and not allow page rank to flow as this is not an editorial link.

Example:

<a href="..." rel="nofollow">click here</a>

"Unnatural links from your site"

Cause: Selling text links on your website for the purpose of passing link juice.

Symptom: Sites are usually not affected initially but failing to take corrective action may lead to a 20-40% drop in your website traffic.

Treatment: Google is not against advertising as such, after all many sites rely on this type of revenue stream, but they do not tolerate the selling of text links that pass on link juice.

The solution to this notice is simple. Either remove the links from your site, or add a *"rel=nofollow"* parameter to the links anchor tag, preventing the passing of link juice, and the problem will be solved.

"Hacked site"

Cause: The website in question has been attacked by Malware, a Virus, a Trojan, or any other hack, including the hijacking of your page(s) or entire site.

Symptom: Doom and disaster resulting in almost 100% drop in website traffic.

Treatment: Replace the contents of your site with a valid backup, or contact your web hosting company who may be able to clean up the Malware for you. If your website gets attacked or compromised frequently you should consider upgrading your CMS or backend system to the latest version, or move to a more secure server.

"Cloaking & Sneaky redirects"

Cause: Cloaking is the practice of showing a different version of page contents to Googlebot than you would for a normal visitor in an attempt to trick Google with keyword rich content, while showing a lighter, more readable version to the visitor. The use of doorway pages can also prompt the issue of this notice.

Symptom: A 20-40% drop in organic traffic. The pages that employ the above cloaking technique will likely be dropped from the search engine index

Treatment: Remove the problem pages and create fresh pages with unique quality content. Use the "Fetch as Google" option in webmaster tools to check if the contents are served exactly the same to the end user as they are to Google.

"Hidden text and/or keyword stuffing"

Cause: Trying to cheat Googlebot with hidden text techniques in the form of hidden layers, divisions or by the use of camouflage (white text on a white background for example). This notice can also be caused by the excessive use of keywords only for the sake of optimization, and serving no benefit or value to a normal user.

Symptom: Affected page(s) or even the entire site may be de-indexed by Google.

Treatment: Check the keyword density of your pages and make sure keywords are not over 3-4% of your total text. Use the "Fetch as Google" and see if there is hidden content. Remove any offending content and send a reconsideration request (see next section).

"Pure SPAM"

Cause: Content that search engines consider to be useless junk; Spun content (an existing article that has been processed to use different words that mean the same, in an effort to make the article look unique to search engines), scraped content (content obtained from other websites), automatically generated keyword loaded gibberish, and translated content by automated tools.

Symptom: Usually results in a 100% drop in traffic.

Treatment: There appears to be no definitive solutions to this particular problem as these practices are considered the worst offences by major search engines and there is little chance these sites can earn the trust again.

However, before giving up completely and starting over fresh with a new website on a new domain, it would make sense to replace all of your pages with high quality, useful content, and submit a comprehensive reconsideration request. Even if your reconsideration request is successful you should prepare yourself for something of a wait while you earn back trust before expecting a return to your previous rankings.

Recovery & Reconsideration

Disavow Bad Links

Before using the *Disavow Tool*, you are expected to make every effort to have bad links removed on your own. Only after there is a "small fraction" of links left to remove, should one use the tool.

Google has made it clear that using the disavow tool is an act of last resort. They are looking to see that you put in at least as much effort into cleaning up a bad link profile as went into creating it. Simply dumping all of your links into a file and uploading it to the Disavow Links tool is unlikely to get the job done when used in this way.

Manual penalty recovery and Penguin algorithmic recovery are both appropriate uses of this tool. If you were hit by Penguin, and know or think you have bad links, you should probably use this tool.

When contacting webmasters to request the removal of a link, the most effective emails are personalized and don't require any thought on the part of the recipient. Let the webmaster know where the link is positioned on the page, the anchor text and where it points. By including those details, you will be perceived as human and make it easy for the webmaster to find and remove the link.

Warning: There has been a recent trend of webmasters demanding payment for a link removal. Don't do it. Simply document the demand for payment in your Disavow file as a comment and add the link address to be removed.

The Link Disavow tool is designed for SEOs and is not linked directly via webmaster tools. You can access the tool here:

https://www.google.com/webmasters/tools/disavow-links-main

Log into Google Webmaster Tools, then go to the Disavow Tool via the link above and select your domain from the list.

Clicking *Disavow Links* will produce a menu asking you for a file containing the links you wish to disavow. This is the list of any remaining links that you could not get removed manually. Upload the file and you're done.

Your file needs to be in plain text format (a .txt file) and encoded as UTF8 or ANSI7 format. Each entry should appear on a new line and either contains the full URL of the offending link, or to block an entire domain simply precede the domain name with the string '*domain:*'

You can also add comments to your disavow file by starting the line with a # character as in the example file below:

Example:

 # requests to remove links on this domain ignored
domain:needsblocking.com

 # no response to removal requests
http://www.somesite.com/page.html

 # domain demanding payment for link removal
domain:anothersite.com

Reconsideration Requests

Once all the hard work of link removal is out of the way and you're confident you have done as much as you can to remove bad links, it's time to submit a reconsideration request.

If you suspect your site has suffered some form of penalty but unsure of whether it's manual or algorithmic, submitting a reconsideration request would be your best way to find out. You can speculate, but why not just go to Google and ask? As with the disavow tool, there is no direct access via webmaster tools. You can get access to the reconsideration page here:

http://www.google.com/webmasters/tools/reconsideration

Only if you have suffered a manual penalty will you need to file a reconsideration request. When filing your request, here are some key points to consider:

- Be specific – Clearly state the steps you have taken to fix the problem and comply with webmaster guidelines.
- Confess everything – Do not attempt top hide anything, be honest.
- Accept responsibility – Explain why this issue will NEVER happen again, e.g. bad SEO advice.

***

APPENDIX A - SEO GLOSSARY

SEO Glossary of Terms

We have compiled a useful *glossary* of common terms used in this book as well as within the Search Engine Optimization (SEO) and Internet Marketing industry. Use this resource while conducting SEO related research on the internet to avoid confusion with some of the many terms and acronyms used in the industry.

301 Redirect - A permanent server redirect of a web page address often found in the htaccess file on Apache servers, or within server side scripts, also useful for dealing with duplicate content issues.

Adwords - Google's pay per click contextual advertisement program, a common source of basic website monetization and advertisement.

Affiliate - An affiliate site markets products or services that are actually sold and delivered by another website or business in exchange for a commission or other benefits.

Algorithm (algo) - A system used by search engines to determine what pages to suggest, and in what order, for a given search term or query.

Alt Text - A text description of a graphic, usually not shown to the end user, unless the image is not available, or a browser is used that does not support images. Alt text is important because search engines cannot read images and rely on this text to obtain an accurate description for the graphic object.

Analytics - A program that assists webmasters in gathering and analyzing data about website usage and trends. Google analytics is a feature rich, free analytics program.

Anchor Text - The visible, clickable text of a web page link. Search engines use anchor text to indicate the relevancy of the referring website, and the link to the content on the target page. Ideally all three will have some keywords in common.

Authority - The amount of trust that a website is given, for a particular search term, or query. Authority is derived largely from related incoming links from other trusted authority sites.

Authority Site - A website that has many incoming links from other related hub sites. Because of this simultaneous citation from trusted expert sites and hubs, an authority site usually has high trust, Pagerank, and search results placement.

Backlink (back link, incoming link) - Any incoming link to a page or website from any other page or website.

Black Hat – Those non-ethical search engine optimization techniques that are counter to establishing best practices such as the Google Webmaster Guidelines. Link spam and keyword stuffing are good examples.

Blog (web-log) - A website that often presents content in a chronological way. Content may, or may not, be time sensitive. Most blogs use a Content Management System rather than individually crafted pages. Because of this, the blogger can concentrate his efforts on content creation instead of coding.

Bot (robot, spider, crawler) - A program, or application, that performs a task autonomously. Search engines use bots to find, read and add web pages to their indexes.

Bounce Rate - The percentage of users who enter a site and then leave it without viewing any other pages.

Bread Crumbs (breadcrumbs) - A type of web site navigation, usually in a horizontal bar above the main content that helps the user to understand where they are in relation to other pages on the site.

Canonical (duplicate content) - It is often nearly impossible to avoid duplicate content, especially with the use of CMSs, but also due to the fact that www.xyz.com, xyz.com, and www.xyz.com/index.htm are often seen as duplicates by the SEs. These issues can be dealt with in several ways including; the use of the noindex meta tag in the non-canonical copies, and 301 server redirects to the master.

Click Fraud - Clicks on a PPC advertisement, usually by the publisher or his friends, for the purpose of undeserved profit.

Cloak - Delivering different content to a search engine spider than would be delivered to a human user. This *black hat* technique is frowned upon by the search engines, and where detected could result in a virtual death penalty of the site/domain being banned fro SERPs.

CMS - Content Management System; Programs such as Wordpress, which separate most of the Webmaster tasks like coding, from content creation so that a publisher can create content without acquiring any specialist coding skills.

Code Swapping (bait and switch) - Changing the page content after a high search engine ranking is achieved.

Comment Spam - Posting social, blog or forum comments for the express purpose of generating a link to another site. The reason many blogs now use *nofollow* links.

Content (text, copy) - The part of a web page that is intended to have value for the end user. Ads, navigation, headers, footers, and branding are not usually considered as content.

Contextual Advertisement - Advertising that is related to the topic of the page content in which it is shown.

Conversion (goal) – Measures the achievement of a specific goal, or target, on a business website. Ad clicks, sign-ups, and sales are examples of conversions.

Conversion Rate - Percentage of users that convert into sales or leads - See *conversion*.

CPC - Cost per click; the rate that is paid per click on a Pay Per Click Advertisement.

CPM - Cost per thousand impressions; a metric used to quantify the average value and cost of Pay Per Click advertisements, with 'M' taken from the Roman numeral for one thousand.

Crawler (bot, spider) - A program that navigates through the web, or a website, using links to gather data on the content it encounters.

Directory - A website devoted to directory listing pages. The *Yahoo* directory and *Dmoz* (open directory project) are good examples.

Directory Page - A page located within a directory site that contains links to other related, or categorized, web pages and websites.

Doorway (gateway) - A web page designed specifically to attract high levels of traffic from search engines.

Duplicate Content - Content that is similar, or identical to, the content found on another website or web page. A site serving duplicate content may well receive little, if any, trust from search engines compared to the content that the SE considers to be the original.

E-commerce Site - A website devoted to online retail sales.

Feed - Content that is delivered to the user via special websites or programs such as news readers.

FFA (free for all) - A website with many outgoing links to unrelated sites, that contain little, if any, unique content. Only intended for spiders, and have little value to human users, and so are often ignored or penalized.

Frames - An outdated web page design where two or more documents appear on the same screen, each within it's own space or 'frame'. Frames are not so good for SEO purposes because spiders often fail to correctly navigate and index sites with this structure.

Gateway Page (doorway) - A page designed to attract traffic from search engines, and then redirect it to another site or page. A doorway page is not identical to cloaking, but the effect is the same; end users and search engines are served different content.

Gizmo (gadget, widget) - A small application used on web pages to provide specific functions such as a hit counter. Gizmos can make good *link bait*.

Google Bomb - The combined effort of multiple webmasters to change the search results, usually for humorous effect. The *"miserable failure" - George Bush*, is a famous example.

Google Bowling (negative SEO) - Maliciously trying to lower a web site rank of a competitor by sending it links from a "bad neighborhood". There is some controversy over negative SEO and if this actually works.

Google Dance - 1) The change in SERPs position caused by an update of the Google database or algorithm, a cause of great angst for many webmasters who slip in the SERPs. 2) The period during a Google update when different data centers hold different data.

Google Juice (trust, authority, pagerank) - Trust / authority from Google, that flows through outgoing links and passed on to other web pages.

Googlebot - Googles web page spider program. Used for crawling websites and indexing web pages.

GYM - Google, Yahoo and Microsoft, the top three major search engines.

Hub (expert page) - A trusted page with *high quality* topical content that links to other quality related pages.

HTML (Hyper-Text Markup Language) - Embedded directives or "markup" which are used to add special web formatting and functionality to plain text for use as pages on the internet.

Impression (page view) - The event when an individual user views a web page, a single time.

Inbound Link (inlink, incoming link) - Inbound links from related pages are the source of *trust* and *pagerank* and important in terms of search engine optimization.

Index (Noun) - A database of web pages and their associated content used by a search engine.

Index (Verb) - To add a web page or resource to a search engine index.

Indexed Pages - The page(s) on a website that have been indexed by the search engine.

Keyword (key phrase) - A word or phrase that a user enters into a search engine to find relevant results.

Keyword Cannibalization - The excessive use of identical keywords on too many pages within the same site. This makes it difficult for end users and the search engines to determine what page is most relevant for a particular keyword.

Keyword Density - Represents the percentage of words on a web page which are a particular keyword. If this value is unnaturally high the page may be penalized for keyword stuffing.

Keyword Research - The hard work of determining keywords that are appropriate for targeting a particular web page.

Keyword Spam (keyword stuffing) - Used to describes an inappropriately high keyword density.

Landing Page - The web page that a search engine user lands on when they click on a link within a SERP.

Latent Semantic Indexing (LSI) - This just means that the search engines index commonly associated groups of words in a page or document. SEO professionals refer to these groups of terms as "Long Tail Keywords". Most searches consist of at least three or more words strung together as a phrase. See *Long Tail*.

Link - An element on a web page that may be clicked on to cause the browser to navigate to another page, or another part of the current web page.

Link Bait - A web page with the designed purpose of attracting incoming links, often via social media.

Link Building - The tasks of actively cultivating new incoming links to a web site or page, in order to improve rankings.

Link Condom - Any of several methods used to avoid passing link juice to another website or web page, to avoid detrimental results of endorsing a bad website by way of an outgoing link, or to discourage link spam in user generated content and comments.

Link Exchange - A reciprocal linking scheme often used by directories. Link exchanges usually allow links to sites of little or no quality, and add no value themselves. Quality directories are usually human edited for quality assurance.

Link Farm - A group of websites that all link to each other.

Link Juice (trust, authority, pagerank) - A Google assigned value passed to an outgoing link.

Link Love - An outgoing link, which is allowed to pass trust and page rank, without any type of link condom.

Link Partner (link exchange, reciprocal linking) - Two separate sites which link to each other in a mutual fashion. Search engines will not usually see these links as high value, because of their reciprocal nature.

Link Popularity - A measurement of the value of a site based upon the number and quality of websites that link to it.

Link Spam (comment spam) - Unwanted links such as those posted in user generated content like blog comments and forum posts.

Link Text (anchor text) – This is the user visible text part of a hyperlink. Search engines use anchor text to indicate the relevancy of the referring site and the content on the landing page. Ideally all three should share some keywords in common.

Long Tail - Longer, more specific search queries that are often less targeted than shorter broad queries. For example a search for "widgets" might be very broad while "blue widgets with round ends" would be a long tail search. A large percentage of searches are long tail.

Mashup - A page that consists primarily of single purpose software and other small programs (gizmos and gadgets), or possibly links to such programs. Mashups are quick and easy to produce and are often popular with users, making them ideal link bait.

META Tags - Entries within the HEAD section of an HTML page that provide information about the page contents. META information may be in the SERPs but is not usually visible on the page. It is very important to have unique and accurate META title and description tags, because they may be the information that the search engines rely upon the most to determine the topic of a page.

Metric - A standard of measurement used by analytics programs.

MFA - Made for advertisements; websites that are designed from the ground up as a venue for placing advertisements.

Mirror Site - An identical site with identical content located at a different web address.

Monetize - To extract income from a web site using advertising, affiliate programs, direct sales etc. Adsense ads are an easy way to monetize a website.

Natural Search Results (organic) - The standard search engine results which are not sponsored, or paid for in any way.

Nofollow - The 'nofollow' command is found in either the HEAD section of a web page or within individual link code, which instructs robots to not follow either any links on the page or the specific link. This is a type of *link condom*.

Noindex - The 'noindex' command is found in either the HEAD section of a web page or within individual link code that instructs robots to not index a web page or the specific link.

Non Reciprocal Link - If website A links to website B, but B does not link back to A, then it is considered a non reciprocal link. Search engines tend to give more value to non-reciprocal links than to reciprocal ones because they are less likely to be the result of collusion between the two sites.

Organic Link - Organic links are those that are natural and published only because the webmaster considers them to add value for users.

Outlink - An out going link to another external website.

Pagerank (PR) - A value assigned by the Google algorithm that represents link popularity and trust among other (proprietary) ranking factors.

Pay For Inclusion (PFI) - The practice of charging a fee to include a website in a search engine or directory. While quite common, usually what is paid for is faster consideration and inclusion, to avoid Google's ban on paid links.

Portal - A website or service that offers a wide range of features and benefits to entice users to make the portal their "home page". Yahoo and MSN are examples of web portals.

PPA (Pay per Action) - Similar to Pay Per Click (PPC) except publishers only get paid when a click through results in certain actions or result in conversions.

PPC (Pay per Click) - An advertising scheme where advertisers pay ad agencies when a unique end user clicks on their ad. Adwords is an example of PPC advertising.

Proprietary Method (bull, snake oil) - A sales term often used by SEO service providers to imply that they can do something unique to achieve "Top 10 Rankings" in SERPS (only the CEO of Google could make such a claim).

Reciprocal Link (link exchange, link partner) - Two websites that mutually link to one another. Search engines usually don't see these as high value links, due to the reciprocal nature.

Redirect - Any one of several methods used to change the web address of a web page, such as when a site is moved to a new domain, or in the case of a doorway page.

Regional Long Tail (RLT) - A multiple keyword phrase that containing a city, or region name. These are especially useful for conducting SEO in the service industry.

Robots.txt - A file named 'robots.txt' located in the root directory of a website, used to restrict and control the behavior of search engine spiders and robots.

ROI (return on investment) - One use of web analytics software is to analyze and quantify your return on investment, and so the cost and benefit of different marketing efforts.

Sandbox - There has been debate and speculation that Google puts all new sites into a "sandbox," preventing them from ranking well for any search terms until a set period of time has passed.

Scrape - The act of copying content (scraping) from another website, often facilitated by automated bots.

SE - Search Engine (see below).

Search Engine (SE) - An application that searches a document or group of documents for relevant matches for a user's keyword phrase and returns a list of the most relevant matches. Major search engines such as Google and Yahoo search the entire internet for relevant results.

Search Engine Spam - Web pages designed to cause search engines to deliver less relevant results. SEOs are sometimes unfairly labeled as search engine Spammers. Of course, in some cases they actually are.

SEM - Search engine marketing; often used to describe acts associated with the researching, submitting and ranking of a Website within search engines to achieve maximum exposure of the site. SEM includes things tasks like search engine optimization, paid listings and other search related functions that will increase traffic to your Web site.

SEO - Search engine optimization; term used to describe the process of increasing the traffic (visitors) to a website by achieving high ranking in search result pages. The higher a website ranks in the results of a search, the greater the chance that users will visit the site. SEO helps to ensure that a site is search engine friendly and improves the chances that the site will be favorably ranked.

SERP - Search engine results page; the results shown to a user after entering a keyword phrase or search term.

Site Map - A page (or group of pages) that link to all accessible pages on a website, clarifying the data structure for the site users. An XML sitemap is also often located in the root directory of a site to help search engines find and index all pages on a site.

SMM (social media marketing) - Website, business or brand promotion through social media sites such as twitter and Facebook.

Social Bookmark - A form of *Social Media*, where a user can bookmark a website, and these bookmarks are made available for public access.

Social Media - Online sources used by people to share information and perspectives. Blogs, wikis, forums, social bookmarking, user reviews and rating sites (digg, reddit) are all examples of Social Media.

Social media marketing (SMM) :: Website, business or brand promotion conducted via social media websites.

Spammer - A person or body that uses spam techniques to pursue a goal.

Spider (bot, crawler) - A specialized bot used by search engines to find and add web pages to their indexes.

Splash Page – Graphical oriented page containing no significant text content. Splash pages are intended to look good to real people but without attention to SEO may look like dead ends to search engine spiders that only read text and links.

Static Page - A web page containing no dynamic content or variables like session IDs within the URL. Static pages are good for SEO purposes as they are very friendly to search engine spiders.

Stickiness - Mitigation of bounce rate. Pages that entice a user to stay longer, and view more pages, improve the website's *stickiness*.

Submission - The act of submitting or suggesting a website or web page(s) for inclusion in a search engine indexes or directories.

Supplemental Index (supplemental results) - Pages with very low pagerank, but are still relevant to a search query, often appear in the SERPs with a label of *Supplemental Result.*

Text Link - A plain HTML link containing only text, and does not involve graphics or special code such as JavaScript.

Time On Page - The amount of time a user spends on a single web page, before moving away. This can be an indication of quality and relevance.

Toolbar Pagerank (PR) - A value between 0 and 10 assigned by the Google algorithm, one that quantifies a pages importance and is not the same as pagerank. Toolbar Pagerank is only updated a several times a year, and is not a reliable indicator of overall trust or authority.

Trust Rank - A method of differentiating between pages with value and spam pages by quantifying link relationships from trusted human vetted seed pages.

URL - Uniform Resource Locator; The full address of a web page or resource (as seen in the address bar of a web browser).

User Generated Content (UGC) - Social Media, wikis, forums and some blogs rely heavily on User Generated Content.

Web 2.0 - Characterized by websites that encourage user interaction.

White Hat - SEO techniques that conform to best practice guidelines, and do not attempt to game or manipulate SE result pages.

Widget - 1) (gadget, gizmo) small programs used on web pages to provide specific functions such as a hit counter. 2) a term borrowed from economics which means "any product or commodity".

APPENDIX B - ISO LANGUAGE CODES

ISO 639-1 is a standard that defines abbreviations for different languages. In HTML and XHTML they can be used in the *lang* and *xml:lang* attributes to specify the language of a web page.

Abkhazian	ab	Afar	aa
Afrikaans	af	Albanian	sq
Amharic	am	Arabic	ar
Aragonese	an	Armenian	hy
Assamese	as	Aymara	ay
Azerbaijani	az	Bashkir	ba
Basque	eu	Bengali	bn
Bhutani	dz	Bihari	bh
Bislama	bi	Breton	br
Bulgarian	bg	Burmese	my
Byelorussian	be	Cambodian	km
Catalan	ca	Chinese	zh
Chinese (S)	zh-Hans	Chinese (T)	zh-Hant
Corsican	co	Croatian	hr
Czech	cs	Danish	da
Dutch	nl	English	en
Esperanto	eo	Estonian	et
Faeroese	fo	Farsi	fa
Fiji	fj	Finnish	fi
French	fr	Frisian	fy
Galician	gl	Gaelic (S)	gd
Gaelic (M)	gv	Georgian	ka
German	de	Greek	el
Greenlandic	kl	Guarani	gn
Gujarat I	gu	Haitian Creole	ht
Hausa	ha	Hebrew	he iw
Hindi	hi	Hungarian	hu

Icelandic	is	Ido	io
Indonesian	id in	Interlingua	ia
Interlingue	ie	Inuktitut	iu
Inupiak	ik	Irish	ga
Italian	it	Japanese	ja
Javanese	jv	Kannada	kn
Kashmiri	ks	Kazakh	kk
Kinyarwanda	rw	Kirghiz	ky
Kirundi (Rundi)	rn	Korean	ko
Kurdish	ku	Laothian	lo
Latin	la	Latvian (Lettish)	lv
Limburgish	li	Lingala	ln
Lithuanian	lt	Macedonian	mk
Malagasy	mg	Malay	ms
Malayalam	ml	Maltese	mt
Maori	mi	Marathi	mr
Moldavian	mo	Mongolian	mn
Nauru	na	Nepali	ne
Norwegian	no	Occitan	oc
Oriya	or	Oromo (Afaan)	om
Pashto (Pushto)	ps	Polish	pl
Portuguese	pt	Punjabi	pa
Quechua	qu	Rhaeto-Romance	rm
Romanian	ro	Russian	ru
Samoan	sm	Sangro	sg
Sanskrit	sa	Serbian	sr
Serbo-Croatian	sh	Sesotho	st
Setswana	tn	Shona	sn
Sichuan	Yi ii	Sindhi	sd
Sinhalese	si	Siswati	ss
Slovak	sk	Slovenian	sl
Somali	so	Spanish	es
Sundanese	su	Swahili (Kiswahili)	sw
Swedish	sv	Tagalog	tl
Tajik	tg	Tamil	ta

Tatar	tt	Telugu	te
Thai	th	Tibetan	bo
Tigrinya	ti	Tonga	to
Tsonga	ts	Turkish	tr
Turkmen	tk	Twi	tw
Uighur	ug	Ukrainian	uk
Urdu	ur	Uzbek	uz
Vietnamese	vi	Volap?k	vo
Wallon	wa	Welsh	cy
Wolof	wo	Xhosa	xh
Yiddish	yi ji	Yoruba	yo
Zulu	zu		

APPENDIX C - USEFUL RESOURCES

Some concepts examined in this book are examined in greater detail on our **Website**, along with alternative formats for this publication, and other books by the author;
http://www.ezwebsitepromotion.com

This easy to use online website analysis tool will produce **Free SEO Report** for any web page on your site. It can help you get started quickly implementing the techniques outlined in this book, simply enter your page URL and keywords.
http://www.ezwebsitepromotion.com/webmasters-tools.asp

Our **Free Templates** to help build your privacy policy and terms of use pages can be found at;
http://www.ezwebsitepromotion.com/templates/

Did you find the information within this book useful? Have a question? Like our page on **Facebook** and leave a comment.
https://www.facebook.com/learn.seo.book

Follow us on **Twitter** for regular useful SEO, Social Media and Internet Marketing tweets.
https://twitter.com/EzWebPromote

Webmaster tools for the major search engines, where you can submit your sitemap and monitor traffic, keywords and other useful data for your website traffic at;

Google
http://www.google.com/webmasters/tools/

Bing
http://www.bing.com/toolbox/

Track your website visitors with *Google Analytics*, a free service providing valuable usage data and metrics.
http://www.google.com/analytics/

Stuck with coding and editing your **HTML** pages? Here is an excellent primer / tutorial to help you on your way.
http://www.htmlprimer.com/htmlprimer/html-primer